KUMIHIMO
WIRE JEWELRY

Essential Techniques and 20 Jewelry Projects
for the Japanese Art of Braiding

GIOVANNA IMPERIA

POTTER
CRAFT

New York

Text and illustrations copyright © 2011
by Giovanna Imperia.

All photographs by Jack Zilker, copyright © 2011 by Potter Craft,
except as follows: page 6: photo by Aya Nakayama; and page 11,
bottom right: photo by Michael Hattori.

Published in 2011 by Potter Craft,
an imprint of the Crown Publishing Group,
a division of Random House, Inc., New York

www.crownpublishing.com

www.pottercraft.com

POTTER CRAFT and colophon is a
registered trademark of Random House, Inc.

Library of Congress Cataloging-in-Publication Data

Imperia, Giovanna.
 Kumihimo wire jewelry : essential techniques and 20 jewelry
projects for the Japanese art of braiding / Giovanna Imperia.
 p.cm.
 Includes index.
 ISBN 978-0-8230-8551-4
 1. Jewelry making—Japan. 2. Wire craft—Japan. 3. Braid—Japan. I.
Title.
 TT212.I55 2011
 739.270952—dc22

 2010013083

Design by Karla Baker
Printed in China
First printing, 2011

1 2 3 4 5 6 7 8 9 / 18 17 16 15 14 13 12 11

DEDICATION

There are many people I would like to thank for their support and faith in this project starting with the kumihimo artists who graciously agreed to contribute some of their work. Without their contributions this book would not have been as exciting:

Shirley Berlin (United Kingdom)

Dominique Brochard (France)

Edna Gibson (United Kingdom)

Michael Hattori (United States)

Anna Hurwitz (United Kingdom)

Sandy Jassett (United Kingdom)

Carole MacAllister (United Kingdom)

Leigh Morris (New Zealand)

Aya Nakayama (Japan)

Maristella Ornati (Italy)

Makiko Tada (Japan)

A special thanks to Pat Powell (United States) and Lidia Musetti (Italy) who also contributed two projects.

I am also thankful to my friends and sensei Rodrick Owen, Makiko Tada, and Masako Kinoshita for their wonderful input and moral support.

I am deeply grateful to my editors, Joy Aquilino and Martha Moran; my photographer, Jack Zilker, and my graphic designer, illustrator, and daughter, Cristina Cook. Without their tireless work, direction, assistance, and guidance this book would not have been possible.

Last but not least, I would like to thank my husband, Lance Cook, who has supported me throughout the many months of hard work.

Giovanna Imperia

GIOVANNA IMPERIA is a fine craft jeweler whose work features various dimensional techniques such as kumihimo and weaving and incorporates wire, fiber, beads, and other mediums. A former artist-in-residence at the Houston Center for Contemporary Craft, she has been teaching workshops on kumihimo since 2001. Her work has been exhibited and is included in private and museum collections throughout the United States and internationally, and she has also been published in various textile and jewelry publications. For more information on Giovanna's work and classes go to giovannaimperiadesigns.com. This is her first English-language book.

Necklace by Aya Nakamaya. For this necklace, Aya Nakayama used a method she developed to harmoniously blend the silver wire into the silk. The result is a seamless flow from the cast centerpiece to the braided wire to the braided silk.

CONTENTS

Bracelets by Giovanna Imperia.

PREFACE

While kumihimo has been around for many centuries, new interest in it has surged in Japan and the West over the last twenty years. Many books have been written on the subject and they have helped popularize the technique, making ku-mihimo more accessible by presenting technically rigorous information in a user-friendly way. Most recently, many small project oriented books have emerged in the United States, all of which, unfortunately, lack the technical knowledge and expertise of the earlier books. This suggested to me the need for a new type of book: A book that would address readers' desires for easy-to-follow projects without compromising on what I consider an essential technical foundation. With these essential techniques, I provide a framework that will help you develop an understanding of basic braid structures in a way that gives you the creative freedom to develop more complex braid structures on your own. By combining these two elements—essential techniques and projects—this book provides more comprehensive coverage than others and can be used by experienced and novice braiders alike.

Equally important, this is the first kumihimo book on braiding with wire. While wire can be used on any of the traditional kumihimo stands, for this first book on the subject I chose to focus on twenty gorgeous, one-of-a-kind projects for the disk/Maru Dai and the square plate.

The projects in this book, as well as many of the contributions from other artists, represent a radical departure from traditional applications of kumihimo and offer a contemporary view of braided jewelry. The instructions are designed to be clear, concise, and easy to follow, and the contributions from other artists will intrigue and inspire you.

GIOVANNA IMPERIA

INTRODUCTION

An example of a contemporary Peruvian sling braid, a practical braid application. Note the various braid structures used throughout and the colorful tassels, which are added afterward.

Braids are common in many cultures, where they have served a wide range of functions—from practical applications to decorations on garments to key elements in religious ceremonies. Some braiding traditions developed independently in different regions, which led to the emergence of unique designs and structures. Some braiding traditions developed as a result of cultural migration. A good example of the latter is the development of kumihimo in Japan.

There are also many different processes that are used in braiding. Some braids are made without the aid of tools. Other braids are made using a stand, typically round, and weighted bobbins. Among the cultures using stands, Japan is unique in that braids are made using a number of specialized stands, not just a round one.

A BRIEF HISTORY OF KUMIHIMO

The term *kumihimo* means intersected threads. It refers to any type of braid executed using the loop-manipulation method (which does not require equipment) or any number of stands.

Kumihimo has very long history in Japan, where some early examples of impressions of braided structures on pottery date back to the Jomon period (8000–300 BC). By the Kofun period (4th–6th centuries), braids had become common thanks in large part to the diffusion of Buddhism. According to research by Masako Kinoshita, many of the early braids, such as the ones in the Shosoin treasure house (Nara period, AD 645–784), were probably executed using the loop-manipulation braiding technique.

Over the centuries, kumihimo became an integral part of the Japanese culture, where it assumed uses that ranged from the functional (such as ties for prayer scrolls or as lacing devices for the samurai armor, which required nearly three hundred silk braids) to the decorative (such as embellishments for Buddhist statues and rosaries as well as obijime, a narrow braided belt that holds the much wider obi in place). Because of its role in Japanese culture, over time, many different pieces of equipment were developed, which helped artisans produce braids faster and of consistent quality while developing new and more complex structures and designs. Automated machines, developed later in the Meiji period (1867–1912), allowed for even faster production. These machines are still in use today, as are five braiding stands: the Maru Dai, Taka Dai, Karakumi Dai, Kaku Dai, and Ayatake Dai.

THE ZEN OF KUMIHIMO

Kumihimo (like all crafts in Japan) was influenced by two Zen aesthetic principles that still shape contemporary Japanese aesthetic sense: the principles of wabi and sabi (or wabi-sabi).

Wabi-sabi represents a comprehensive worldview centered on the idea of *transience*, an aesthetic of imperfect, incomplete beauty—nothing is permanent, nothing is ever fully completed, nothing *can* be perfect. This is considered by many art critics to be the most conspicuous characteristic of Japanese sense of beauty. The concept evolved over time to assume connotations of minimalist and understated elegance. Beauty is found in the simplest objects.

FINDING BEAUTY IN THE PROCESS

The Japanese aesthetic values not only the end product but the process itself. In the case of kumihimo, beauty exists beyond the finished braid—it also exists in the equipment, made of highly refined wood that changes as it develops a patina due to use and age, in the hand movements, and in the rhythmic sound that the tama (bobbins) make when they click against each other.

The beauty of the braid comes from different aspects: from the materials (typically silk) to the structure to color choices to how the braid is used and how it is presented. Color choice is particularly important for the obijime because the braid must coordinate with the obi and the kimono.

A seven-column, sha silk Buddhist kesa (stole) from the late Meiji period. Note the horn ring and silk braid that fasten the cape toga style. It was probably meant for everyday use, as the fabric is not elaborate, is discolored, and is missing the complex knot called Shutara Musubi, which typically hangs from the back of ceremonial kesa. The artisan who wove it, however, took time to create a beautiful, very subtle tone-on-tone design, as you can see in the detail photograph.

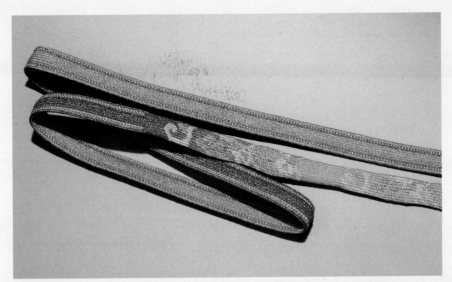

An example of a contemporary obijime found by the author in an exclusive workshop in Kyoto. The obijime was braided on the Taka Dai using a pickup technique to create the design on both sides of the braid. It consists of three layers, which allows a three-color design.

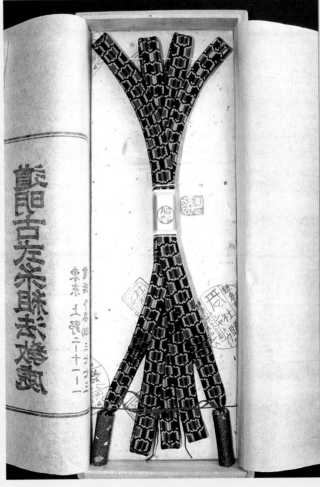

ABOVE An example of contemporary sageo (used to fasten a sword to the waist) in a traditional presentation box. It was created on the Taka Dai by Michael Hattori.

LEFT Necklace by Giovanna Imperia

11

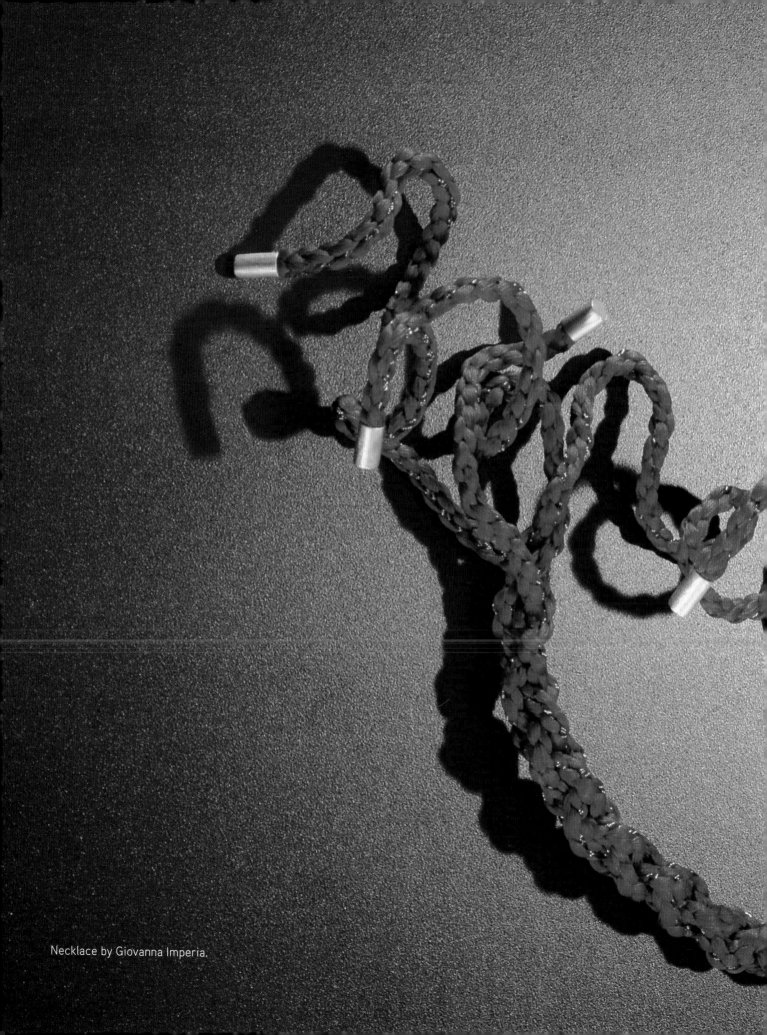

Necklace by Giovanna Imperia.

MATERIALS + TOOLS

FIBER AND OTHER OPTIONS

In Japan, silk has been the fiber of choice for kumihimo for several centuries. Historically, it was measured and dyed by the braider. Today you can buy kumihimo silk in a wide range of colors, precut in standard lengths (primarily 3 and 3.8 yards, appropriate for making obijime and sageo). Small-business artisans produce most kumihimo silk and colors vary from artisan to artisan.

In traditional kumihimo, you do not braid with individual threads but with threads that have been grouped into **bundles**. Four bundles are twisted together to form one rope. Four (or six) ropes are twisted together and packaged for sixteen or twenty-four tama (bobbins). A silk bundle typically consists of forty individual threads. Traditional kumihimo silk is quite fine—similar in size to 2/120 silk or sewing thread—and has a tight ply, which adds strength and sheen.

There are other kumihimo threads available in precut form: artificial silks called shinon or biron (shinon is closest to silk in luster and hand) and metallics. Metallics usually consist of a rayon or nylon core with polyester metallic film wound around it. Metallics are used extensively in the weaving of traditional kimono fabrics and are extremely soft to the touch yet very strong.

Many contemporary kumihimo artists go beyond the precut materials and experiment with a wide range of materials—from plastics and vinyl (like Jelly Yarn®) to horsehair to monofilament to wire—with very interesting results. Ultimately, anything that can be bent can be braided.

BELOW LEFT Precut kumihimo threads in packets premeasured for sixteen or twenty-four tama (bobbins), *clockwise from bottom left:* metallic; variegated silk; shinon (out of the packet), knotted to ensure that threads do not tangle; rope of silk showing the four bundles that form it.

BELOW Contemporary braiding materials, *clockwise from top left:* Jelly Yarn (vinyl), multicolor and black polyurethane with polyester core, cotton coated with polyurethane in three different shapes (thick and thin, round, flat).

WIRE

Any kumihimo braid structure can be executed with wire on any stand or with loop-manipulation, provided that the wire is soft enough and thin enough to be interlaced successfully. Thicker wires can be braided, but they may require a variety of tools, such as torches, hammers, and drawplates. The wires used for the jewelry projects in this book are thin and pliable enough to be worked without special tools.

Wire comes in a wide range of materials, shapes, colors, and thicknesses. Some of the most common shapes available are round, semi-round, square, triangular, and flat. Generally speaking, round wires are the best for braiding.

In the United States, most wire available in craft shops or through jewelry suppliers is measured in gauges. Some American wire is measured in fractions of inches, while fractions of millimeters are used in the rest of the world. A conversion chart of these measuring methods is on page 143; the most common wire thicknesses are show in the chart at right. Note that the higher the gauge number, the thinner the wire. The best gauges for kumihimo are 28-gauge and higher (0.32mm or thinner). A lot of stress is placed on the wire when braiding, and you must use a wire that can survive the manipulation without breaking.

Copper: Copper is one of the best materials for braiding because it is very forgiving—it can be manipulated repeatedly without breaking or becoming work hardened (i.e., stiffer and more brittle as it is worked). In its natural state, copper oxidizes over time and develops a patina, varying from green to dark gray/black.

Copper wire also comes coated and is commonly used in the craft and electronics industries. In electronics it's known as magnet wire or enameled copper wire, and it comes in a range of gauges and large-quantity spools at very affordable prices. The major drawback is that there are only three colors: copper (or natural, coated in a transparent coat), green, and red.

Coated copper wire for the craft industry comes in a range of gauges and many good colors, although not all colors are available in all gauges. The wire gauge is measured *before* coating, so the actual thickness will be different between bare and coated wire of the same gauge. Some finishes are thicker (making the wire stiffer), and some coatings are not very sturdy and tend to break or rub off with use. Sampling and testing is always recommended. Coated copper wire is used in almost every jewelry project in this book.

36 ga.	——————	————	22 ga.
34 ga.	——————	————	20 ga.
32 ga.	——————	————	18 ga.
30 ga.	——————	————	16 ga.
28 ga.	——————	————	14 ga.
26 ga.	——————	————	12 ga.
24 ga.	——————	————	10 ga.

Most common wire thicknesses. Gauge is AWG (American Wire Gauge).

Earrings made of magnet wire by Leigh Morris, using the Edo Yatsu braid structure (page 32).

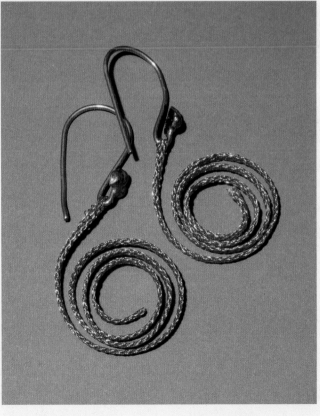

Stainless steel: The lightest of all steel types, it resembles darkened silver or pewter. Musical instrument cords are made of stainless steel because it has memory (it springs back) and resonates when under tension. The springiness can be a challenge when braiding: If not kept under constant tension, it will coil, twist on itself, and become hopelessly tangled. But it is very flexible, braids beautifully, and does not tarnish like silver, bare copper, or brass. With care, it can be soldered and heat colored. It comes in a wide range of gauges, even extremely fine 50- and 60-gauge, and can be found in hardware stores and through industrial suppliers.

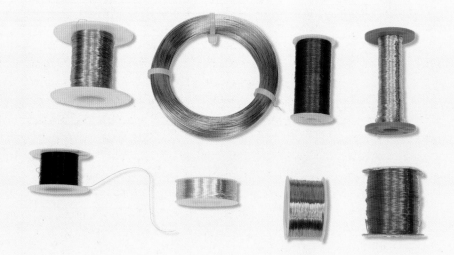

Silver: There are three types: sterling, fine, and Argentium. Of the three, **fine** has the lowest alloy content and is the softest and easiest to braid. Argentium has a different alloy than sterling and does not tarnish or work harden as quickly as sterling, so it is also very suitable for kumihimo.

Gold: The higher the karat, the lower the alloy content and the softer and less likely the wire is to work harden. The karats most suitable for braiding are 18k and 22k.

Aluminum, niobium, and titanium: Niobium and aluminum can be chemically colored (anodized). Aluminum is very soft but perhaps too fragile for braiding jewelry. Niobium is hypoallergenic and develops a bluish tint when exposed to air for extended periods. Like steel and niobium, titanium does not tarnish, is corrosion resistant, and is very strong, but it is lighter than steel.

Iron and brass: These are very-low-cost metals readily available in hardware stores, and they come in a wide range of gauges. Iron is very stiff, and some may find it too hard to braid. (It also rusts easily unless treated.) Brass is stiffer than copper yet very springy, and it can be soldered, electroplated, and heat colored, but it does not offer the same color ranges as copper or steel.

ABOVE Some wires that can be used in kumihimo, *top row from left:* stainless steel spool, stainless steel coil, iron, brass. *Bottom row from left:* 36-gauge coated copper, sterling silver, 30-gauge coated copper, 26-gauge uncoated copper.

BELOW An obijime braided on the Taka Dai by Makiko Tada, who used nickel chromium multifilament steel, a wire used in the automotive industry that is very soft, almost like thread, but extremely strong. Multiple strands of it are twisted or braided together to create a thicker rope.

IMPORTANT DIFFERENCES
BETWEEN FIBER AND WIRE

Wire, no matter how fine, is stiffer and more rigid than fiber. All threads, even non-stretchy ones like linen and silk have some give—they stretch when under tension and relax when not. Wire does neither; it tends to stay exactly where it's placed. Wire interlacements remain more open than thread interlacements unless additional tightening is applied.

While the same process is used to measure wire and thread, they must be handled differently. It is very important to keep wire under tension when measuring and setting up the equipment or it will unravel too quickly from the spool, or twist (kink).

Finished braids made entirely of wire can be reshaped after they are made because wire has memory and is pliable. The same is not true for thread braids; if the braid is uneven it will stay uneven no matter how much manipulating you do.

You may find that working with wire is harder on your hands because you have to pull it more tightly than thread. Take frequent breaks to rest your hands.

BEADS AND EMBELLISHMENTS
FOR FIBER AND WIRE

Many beads and embellishments can be added to a braid either while braiding or afterward using a variety of techniques.

Top row from left: felt beads, size 11 Czech seed beads, vintage French blown-glass seed beads. *Middle row from left:* size E Czech seed beads, size 8 delica beads, two strings of dyed freshwater pearls. *Bottom row from left:* size 6 Japanese seed beads, size 11 Japanese seed beads, size 15 Japanese seed beads.

STANDS, DISKS, AND PLATES

Kumihimo is unique in that braiders can use a number of techniques, many specialized stands, and braiding machines. Over the centuries, various stands were designed to execute specific braid structures, and five of them (Maru Dai, Kaku Dai, Karakumi Dai, Ayatake Dai, Taka Dai) are still used by many contemporary braiders around the world.

MARU DAI

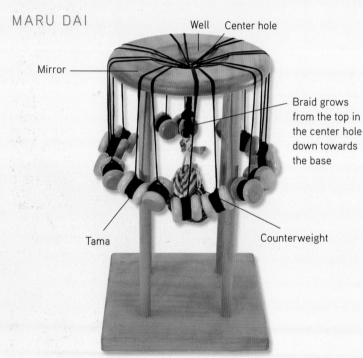

Well   Center hole

Mirror

Braid grows from the top in the center hole down towards the base

Tama

Counterweight

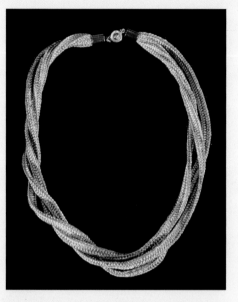

Necklace made on the Maru Dai by Makiko Tada using nickel chromium steel wire.

KAKU DAI

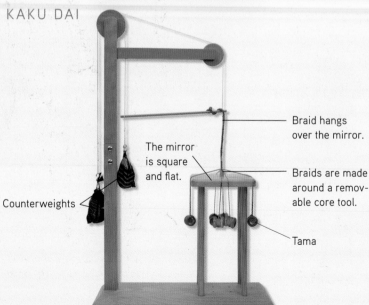

Braid hangs over the mirror.

The mirror is square and flat.

Braids are made around a removable core tool.

Counterweights

Tama

Large silk and wire cuff by Giovanna Imperia. Kaku Dai braids were braided around a sterling silver core and connected to a fabricated sterling frame.

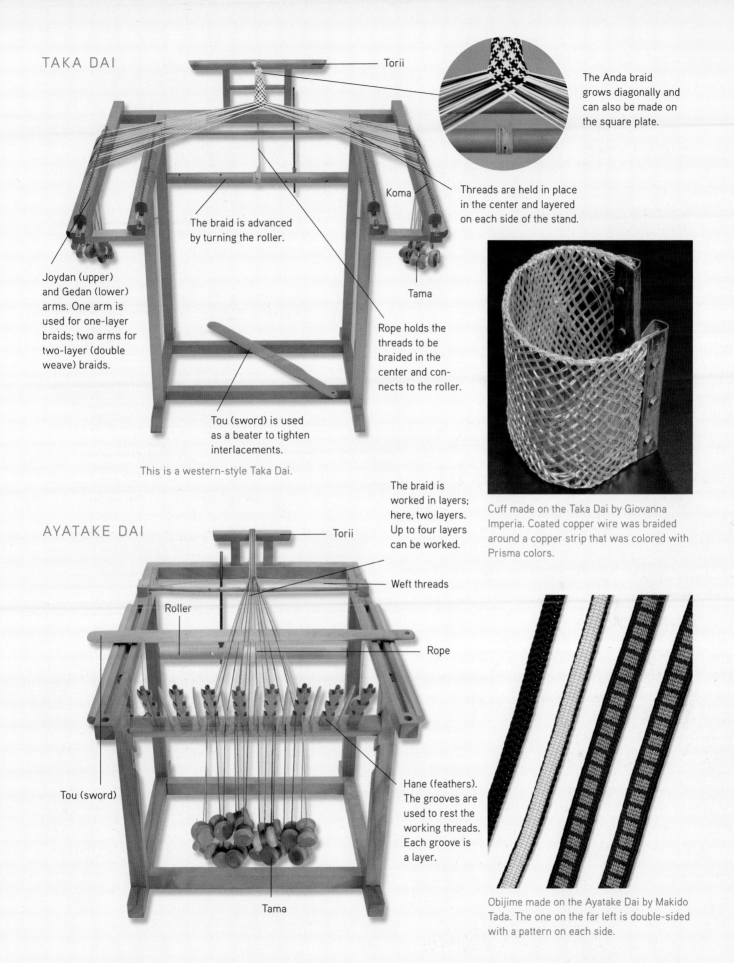

TAKA DAI

Torii

Koma

Tama

The braid is advanced by turning the roller.

Joydan (upper) and Gedan (lower) arms. One arm is used for one-layer braids; two arms for two-layer (double weave) braids.

Rope holds the threads to be braided in the center and connects to the roller.

Tou (sword) is used as a beater to tighten interlacements.

This is a western-style Taka Dai.

The Anda braid grows diagonally and can also be made on the square plate.

Threads are held in place in the center and layered on each side of the stand.

Cuff made on the Taka Dai by Giovanna Imperia. Coated copper wire was braided around a copper strip that was colored with Prisma colors.

AYATAKE DAI

Torii

The braid is worked in layers; here, two layers. Up to four layers can be worked.

Weft threads

Roller

Rope

Tou (sword)

Hane (feathers). The grooves are used to rest the working threads. Each groove is a layer.

Tama

Obijime made on the Ayatake Dai by Makido Tada. The one on the far left is double-sided with a pattern on each side.

KARAKUMI DAI

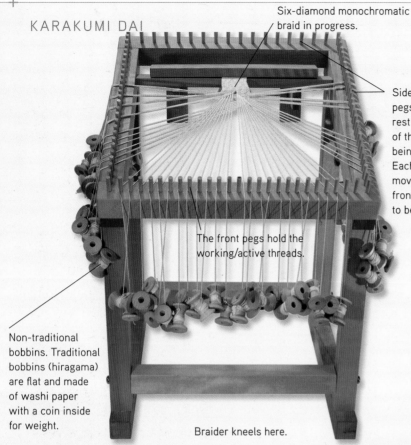

Six-diamond monochromatic braid in progress.

Side and back pegs are used to rest the groups of threads not being worked. Each group moves to the front when ready to be worked.

The front pegs hold the working/active threads.

Non-traditional bobbins. Traditional bobbins (hiragama) are flat and made of washi paper with a coin inside for weight.

Braider kneels here.

An interesting contemporary interpretation of the basic Karakumi structure made by Edna Gibson. Instead of a traditional flat braid, Edna created a textured double-layer braid.

Loop-manipulation braiding: Loop-manipulation braiding requires no tools except for an optional beater (i.e., a person or a foot-activated device to tighten the braid at the point of braiding) when making long braids. At one end, threads are tied together on a fixed support; at the other end, threads are made into loops held by the braider (or multiple braiders). In many cultures, the loops are held in the fingers (the finger-held method); in Oman and Japan, they are held in the hands (hand-held method). To make a braid, loops are exchanged one at a time between the two hands in a predetermined sequence. Based on her extensive research, Masako Kinoshita chose the term *Kute-Uchi* for the particular hand-held technique used in Japan, where hand straps (called Kute) facilitate the interlacement. Kute-Uchi was used continually throughout the Middle Ages and survived until the early modern age. For more information, visit the Loop-manipulation Braiding Research and Information Center founded by Masako Kinoshita (www.lmbric.net).

Bracelet by Sandy Jassett in coated copper wire made using the loop-manipulation braiding technique.

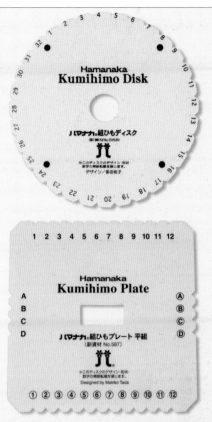

Round disk: The disk is not traditional, it's a recently developed tool that makes kumihimo created on the Maru Dai more accessible. The disk is the same shape as the Maru Dai mirror, and any Maru Dai braid structure can be executed on it.

The disk can be made of many different materials, including cardboard, but Makiko Tada designed one made of very strong yet flexible polyethylene foam, produced in Japan by Hamanaka. It has thirty-two slots that hold threads or wire firmly in place. Often braiders wind the thread or wire on soft bobbins called EZ Bobs to keep them separated and tangle free.

Square plate: The plate is a more recent invention of Makiko Tada, designed to replicate a basic Taka Dai braid structure called Anda (plain). Though only one structure can be done on the plate, you can make many variations of it depending on how the threads are moved and whether the plate is rotated during moves. The plate also offers the flexibility of incorporating a variety of techniques from other crafts (such as the use of short rows, as in knitting). There are twelve numbered slots at the top and the bottom and four lettered slots on each side that hold the thread or wire firmly in place. EZ Bobs will keep thread and wire tangle free.

Here are the disk (top) and the plate (above), which you will use for the projects in this book. Details on how to set them up and braid on them are on pages 39–44.

BRAIDING AND FINISHING SUPPLIES

Here are the tools and supplies you'll need to braid on the Maru Dai, disk, or plate. Details are on pages 39 and 45.

MEASURING AND SETTING UP

Inexpensive scissors

Inexpensive thread

S hook

Chopstick

Small weights

Warping pegs

C-clamps

Measuring tape

EZ Bobs

Tama (Maru Dai)

Counterweight (Maru Dai)

Counterweight bag (Maru Dai)

FINISHING

Ball-peen hammer

Mallet (wood or leather)

Chain-nose pliers

Flat-nose pliers

Round-nose pliers

Wire cutters

Mill file

Jeweler's saw

Mill file(s)

Small anvil or steel block

Wood block

V-bench with clamp

Various grits of sandpaper

End caps and clasps

Headpins

16- or 18-gauge sterling silver wire

Sterling silver tubing

Permanent black marker

Glue

Two-part epoxy resin

Color pigments

Wax paper

Spray finish

Necklace by Giovanna Imperia.

BRAIDING BASICS

MARU DAI and ROUND DISK BASICS

The Maru Dai and the disk are one and the same: every single braid you can do on the Maru Dai you can do on the disk and vice versa. The only major difference between the two is that, because it is not held in one hand like the disk, the Maru Dai allows you to use *both* hands simultaneously so you can move two (or more) threads at the same time.

Reading diagrams: The instruction diagrams for both the Maru Dai and the disk precisely replicate looking down on the devices from the point of view of the braider, as the diagrams below illustrate.

The round Hamanaka disk, which will be used for all of the round disk projects in this book, was specifically designed to allow you to go seamlessly back and forth from the Maru Dai to the disk. If you draw lines connecting the dots on the disk through the center hole, you create the same four sections that are used in the Maru Dai diagrams to help you visualize the correct position of the threads or wires.

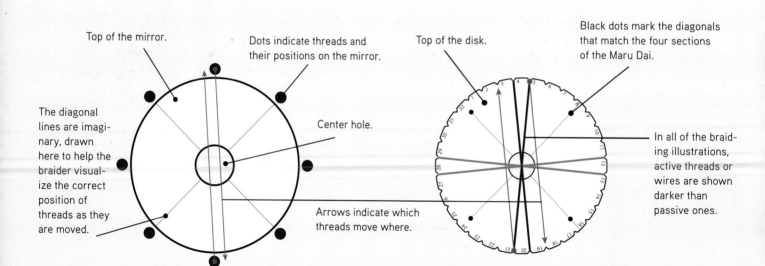

Top of the mirror.

Dots indicate threads and their positions on the mirror.

The diagonal lines are imaginary, drawn here to help the braider visualize the correct position of threads as they are moved.

Center hole.

Arrows indicate which threads move where.

Top of the disk.

Black dots mark the diagonals that match the four sections of the Maru Dai.

In all of the braiding illustrations, active threads or wires are shown darker than passive ones.

MARU DAI MIRROR: It helps to associate the dots representing the threads with the points on a compass (N, S, E, and W). The braider is always in the S position.

ROUND DISK: Braider holds the disk with the numbers between 1 and 8 on the North and between 17 and 24 on the South.

Point of braiding: It is important to pay attention to the point of braiding—how the threads or wires look when the interlacement sequence for a braid structure is completed. The point of braiding is what you see in the center hole of the disk or the Maru Dai (where the braid is formed) when you look down on it. Because threads and wires can be moved in a number of ways, each braid has its own point of braiding. We show the point of braiding for each practice braid in this section and in all the projects. Knowing how a point of braiding is supposed to look can help you figure out right away if a mistake has been made. Always hold the disk so you clearly see the center hole, and sit at the Maru Dai so you can see the center of the mirror.

Practicing with thread: When learning to braid, it is better to use thread than wire, because thread is easier to manipulate and tighten, allowing you to focus on the structures you are learning. You can use any thread you like, but I recommend something thick, like size 8 crochet thread or 10/2 cotton, so you won't need to wind too many strands per slot/Tama—three strands per bobbin should be sufficient.

What you will accomplish: By working through the sample braids on pages 25 to 38, you will learn how to:

- Create various structures by repeating sequences of basic moves in a given pattern
- Create new braids by increasing the number of threads you are working in a given pattern without changing the basic moves used
- Create different structures by changing the position of the threads on the Maru Dai or disk
- Create new structures by combining structures

BASIC MOVES ON THE MARU DAI AND ROUND DISK

To truly understand braid structures, the most important thing is to learn how to place the threads in the correct section of the mirror or disk. If you are working on the disk, it is better to ignore the slot numbers altogether as you practice. You are training your hands to automatically do what your eyes see when they look at the diagram, so the exact slot numbers are not important. Each basic move is shown on both a Maru Dai and round disk diagram, with no written number instructions, so you have to visually match your thread placements to what you see in the diagrams. You may find this a bit challenging at first, but if you go slowly you will soon get the hang of it.

Despite the fact that there are hundreds of documented braiding patterns for the Maru Dai and the disk, they are all created by relying on a set of six basic moves, which can be grouped into two types of interlacements: (1) threads pass over the center hole and (2) threads move around the edge.

THREADS PASS OVER THE CENTER:
BASIC MOVES 1 AND 2

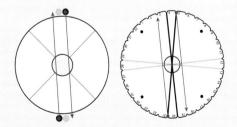

BASIC MOVE 1: Two threads exchange places (one from North [N] section to South [S] section; one from S to N), passing over the center. After the move, you still have the same number of threads in the N and S sections.

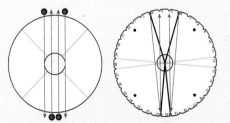

BASIC MOVE 2: Four threads exchange place (two from N to S; two from S to N) passing over the center. After the move, you still have the same number of threads in the N and S sections.

THREADS MOVE AROUND THE PERIMETER:
BASIC MOVES 3–6

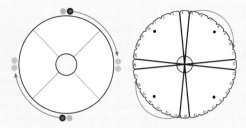

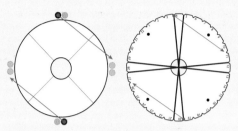

BASIC MOVE 3: The threads in N and S, which are being moved, slide around the perimeter without passing over the center or any other threads. After the move, you have only one thread each in the N and S sections.

BASIC MOVE 4: There is one thread each in the N and S sections. The active threads move around the perimeter while going over *one* passive thread (those not being moved). After the move, you will have only one thread in the N and S sections.

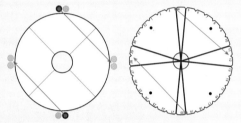

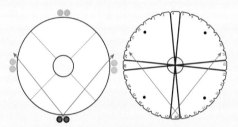

BASIC MOVE 5: One thread from N and one from S move around the perimeter, but here they cross over two passive threads. After the move, you will have only one thread in the N and S sections.

BASIC MOVE 6: The threads are the ones in the S (or N) section. They are crossed over each other and moved to the E and W sections without going over the center. Typically, the left thread crosses over the right. On the disk, the right thread is moved first.

PRACTICE BRAIDS

Different braids are created by repeating the same set of moves with all the threads, or by mixing moves—going over the center with some and going around the perimeter with others. These practice braids, selected to help you understand the mechanics of kumihimo, are merely a few examples of the hundreds you can make with the six basic moves. Some of these braids will be used in the projects, but not all of them.

Practicing these braids will help you understand the structure of a braid as it develops, and understanding structures gives you the flexibility to create more braids on your own.

Some of the sample braids shown here were made with a single color. But if you are having difficulty understanding the movements, use two *contrasting* thread colors, as illustrated in

the diagrams. The braids are shown in Maru Dai diagrams only. If you are using the disk, just move the threads in the positions indicated and don't worry about exact slot numbers. To prepare the thread bundles and set up the disk and Maru Dai, see page 39. You'll understand the structure after braiding 4 to 5 inches (10 to 12 cm), so you'll need no more than 12-inch (30 cm) thread lengths for each sample. Use whatever thread you have handy. The more threads you include in a bundle, the thicker your braid will be and the easier it will be for you to see the structure quickly. These samples were made using DMC embroidery floss—two bundles of six threads per slot.

MARU YOTSU:
THREADS PASS OVER THE CENTER (BASIC MOVE 1)

Maru Yotsu uses only four bundles, one bundle in each section (Maru = round, Yotsu = four).

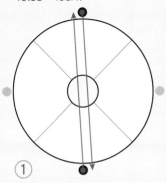

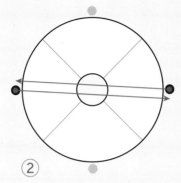

Maru Yotsu point of braiding.

Once you are comfortable with this braid, try this variation: Use the same number of bundles (four), but instead of alternating Move 1 and Move 2, move in this sequence: 1-1-2-2. This structure is used in the Wire and Plastic Necklace on page 105.

Maru Yotsu braid structure.

KUSARI TUNAGI:
THREADS PASS OVER THE CENTER (BASIC MOVE 1)

Kusari Tunagi is a round braid that is actually two four-bundle braids (or two Maru Yotsu). Moves 1 and 2 are exactly the same as for Maru Yotsu. In the diagrams below, you see that we have four green and four blue bundles, each represent-ing a four-bundle braid. The blue bundles (Moves 3 and 4) are moved the exact same way as the green ones. You first braid the green and then braid the blue bundles. The two braids link into each other as a single unit once you go back to Move 1.

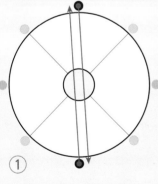

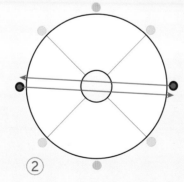

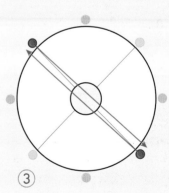

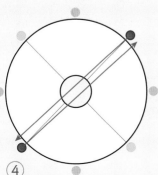

Kusari Tunagi point of braiding.

Kusari Tunagi braid structure.

KONGOH:
THREADS PASS OVER THE CENTER (BASIC MOVE 1)

Kongoh (hardness) is a very strong braid that has many practical applications, from slings to leashes to mountain-climbing ropes. You start with eight bundles (two each in the N, S, E, and W sections). Use two contrasting colors to better see how the braid spirals. The Three Rings project on page 59 uses this structure.

You can choose a clockwise spiral (S spiral) or a counterclockwise one (Z spiral). Pay close attention to which bundles are the active ones and where you lay them. Because it is a spiral, the braid will move around the disk or mirror. You can reposition it after completing each sequence (put the bundles in their original Move 1 places), or allow it to rotate around the disk/mirror. For the latter, it is critical that you ignore the slot numbers and focus on the pairs of threads you are moving.

The bundles are paired, but you only move one bundle from each pair at a time. You move different bundles depending on the direction of your spiral. The move you make with the green bundles is exactly the same move you make with the blue ones. This is important to understand because the moves are the same for all sizes of Kongoh braids—twelve-thread, sixteen-thread, etc. Set up the disk or the Maru Dai then simply repeat the same basic move with each group of bundles. Move 2 is exactly the same as Move 1; you are just using different bundles.

Z SPIRAL

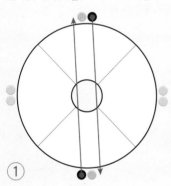

①

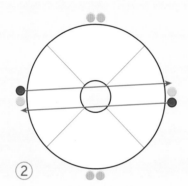

②

Z spiral Kongoh point of braiding.

S SPIRAL

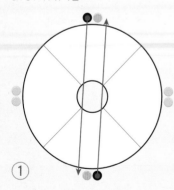

①

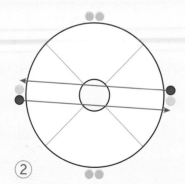

②

S spiral Kongoh point of braiding.

Z spiral Kongah braid structure.

S spiral Kongoh braid structure.

FLAT KONGOH:
THREADS PASS OVER THE CENTER (BASIC MOVE 1)

As you start working with more than eight bundles, you will notice that you can create variations based on how you *position* your threads on the disk or the Maru Dai while still using the same basic moves. With a 12-bundle Kongoh braid like this one, you have one group of eight (blue) bundles in N and S and one group of four (green) bundles in E and W. Because you have more bundles in two sections (N and S) than the others (E and W), the braid will be deformed—instead of being round it will be flat (more precisely, thick and flat), while still spiraling.

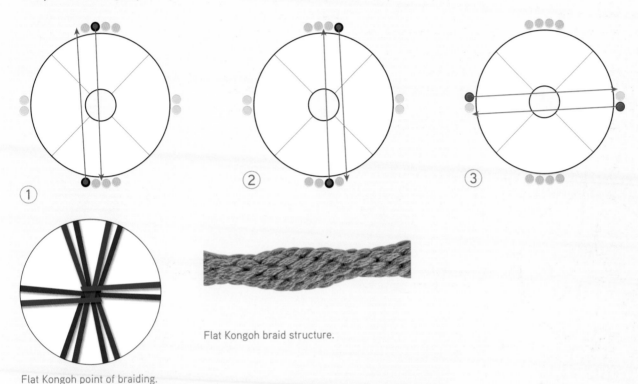

Flat Kongoh braid structure.

Flat Kongoh point of braiding.

Armlet by Giovanna Imperia. Braids are made from coated copper wire in various gauges. The bracelet features multiple Maru Dai structures including Kongoh (dark green braid), set in etched and forged sterling silver.

KUSARI KAKU YATSU:
THREADS PASS OVER THE CENTER (BASIC MOVE 2)

Kusari Kaku Yatsu (Kusari = chain, Kaku = square, Yatsu = eight) is an eight-bundle square braid that looks like a chain. Two pairs of bundles are exchanged on each move.

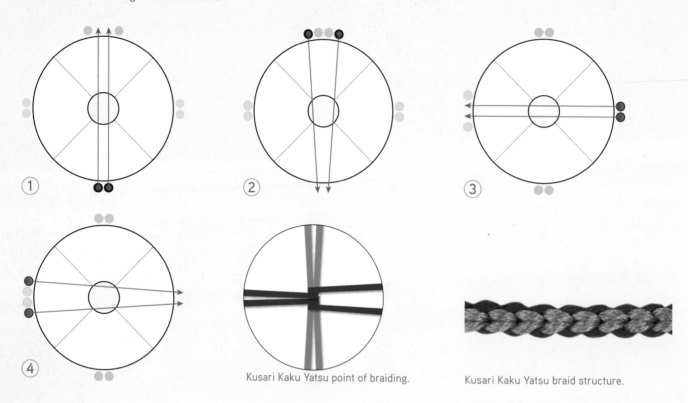

Kusari Kaku Yatsu point of braiding.

Kusari Kaku Yatsu braid structure.

MARU GENJI:
THREADS PASS OVER THE CENTER (BASIC MOVE 2)

As we saw with the Kongoh braid, you can create additional braid structures by simply increasing the number of bundles you braid. Maru Genji is the same as Kusari Kaku Yatsu, but it uses sixteen bundles rather than eight. Because the sixteen bundles are distributed equally in all four sections of the disk or Maru Dai, this braid is round. This structure is used in the Curly Stickpin on page 67.

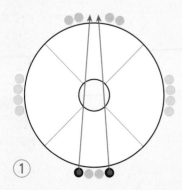
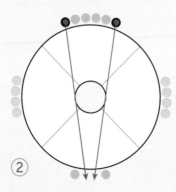
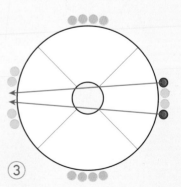

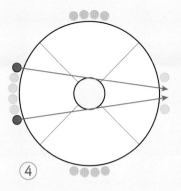

④

Maru Genji point of braiding.

Maru Genji braid structure.

KAKU YATSU:
THREADS MOVE AROUND THE PERIMETER (BASIC MOVE 1)

Kaku Yatsu (Kaku = square, Yatsu = eight) is a square braid with eight bundles. Bundles are typically moved clockwise and then counterclockwise around the perimeter of the disk or Maru Dai. In the first clockwise and counterclockwise moves (Moves 1 and 3), the active bundles (the ones being moved) do not pass over any other bundles. This structure was used in one of the Sampler Bracelets on page 62 and in the Double-Strand Necklace with Large Felted Beads on page 83. You can create more complex braids by working with twice as many bundles (sixteen instead of eight).

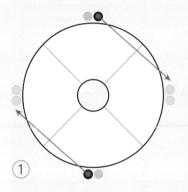

①

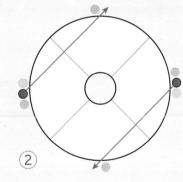

②

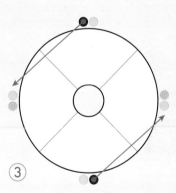

③

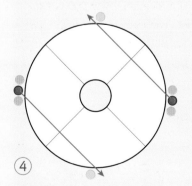

④

Kaku Yatsu point of braiding.

Kaku Yatsu braid structure.

Edo Yatsu (Edo = old name for Tokyo, Yatsu = eight) is an eight-bundle braid. For braids in this category, the active bundles pass over another bundle as they reach their destination. Edo Yatsu and many of the braids in this group are hollow, so they are the best choice when working with cores, but they can also be flattened to create a thicker flat braid. This structure was used for one of the Sampler Bracelets on page 62, the Copper and Black Cuff on page 75, and the Braided Beads Necklace on page 102.

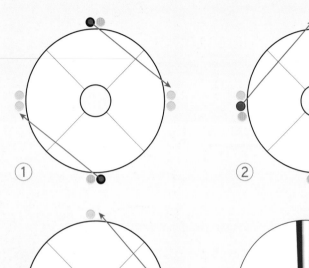

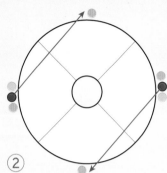

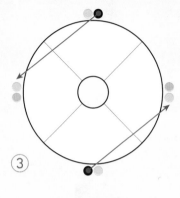

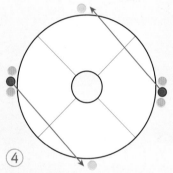

Edo Yatsu point of braiding.

Edo Yatsu braid structure.

It is possible to create more braids by changing the number of times Moves 1–2 and Moves 3–4 are made. For instance, you could do 1-2-1-2 and then 3-4-3-4. You may want to experiment on your own.

Necklace of fine and sterling silver made by Anna Hurwitz using Edo Yatsu and an open zigzag braid structure.

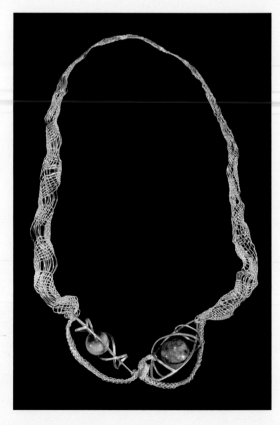

NAIKI:
THREADS MOVE AROUND THE PERIMETER (BASIC MOVE 2)

The Naiki (a proper name) braid is a hollow braid related to the Edo Yatsu but is made using sixteen bundles instead of eight. This structure was used in the Twisted Necklace with Beads (page 79) and the Fresh Water Pearls Necklace on page 87.

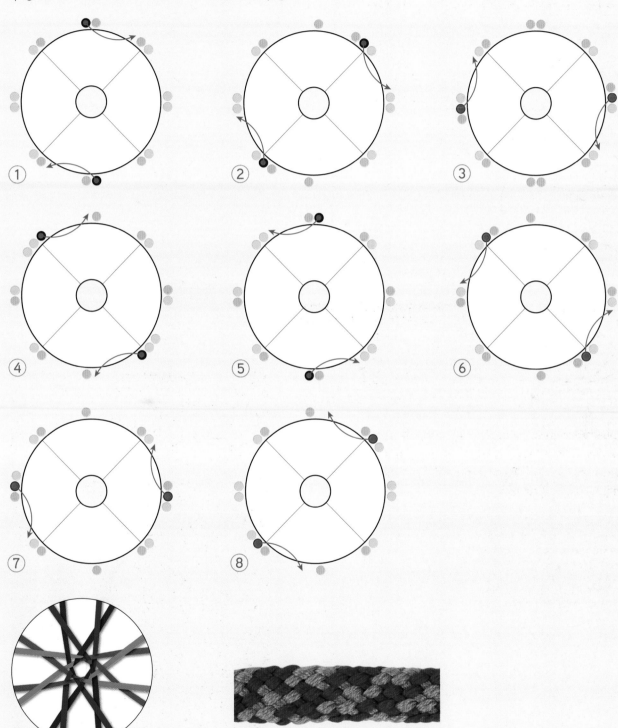

Naiki point of braiding.

Naiki braid structure.

YATSU SE:
THREADS MOVE AROUND THE PERIMETER (BASIC MOVE 4)

Yatsu Se (Yatsu = eight, Se = creek) is an eight-bundle braid. In this category of braids, the active bundles pass over two bundles on their way to their new position. This structure is used in the Single-Braid Bracelet (page 55) and in a twelve-bundle version in the In-and-Out Necklace (page 95).

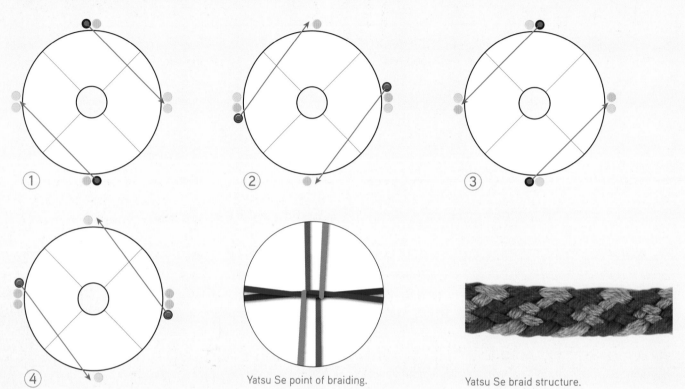

Yatsu Se point of braiding.

Yatsu Se braid structure.

HIRA NAMI:
THREADS MOVE AROUND THE PERIMETER (BASIC MOVE 3)

Hira Nami (Hira = flat, Nami = wave) is a flat, wavy eight-bundle braid. In this category of braids, two bundles are crossed in the first move (typically in the N or S section). A good example of how to do this structure with a larger number of bundles is the Intertwined Braids Bracelet by Lidia Musetti (page 99), where she uses twenty-four bundles.

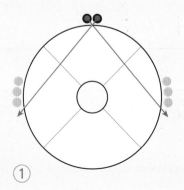
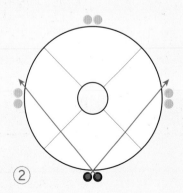
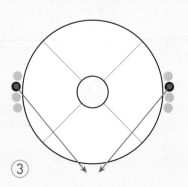

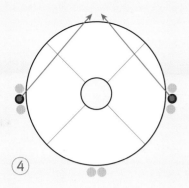

Hira Nami point of braiding.

Hira Nami braid structure.

PUTTING IT ALL TOGETHER:
COMPOUND BRAIDS

In working the practice braids, you've seen how it's possible to create more complex braids by using the same braid structure but increasing the number of bundles being braided (for instance, from eight as in Edo Yatsu to sixteen, as in Naiki) or by placing the bundles differently in the four sections of the disk or the Maru Dai (four bundles in each section, as in the Maru Genji, or four in each of two sections and two in each of the

remaining two sections, as in the Flat Kongoh). Clearly more variations are possible as you increase the number of bundles you work (twenty-four or thirty-two, for instance).

However, it is also possible to create complex braids by combining structures. I call these compound braids. The Lacy Bracelet project on page 71 and the Twisted Necklace with Beads project on page 79 both use compound braids.

Brooch by Lidia Musetti. After the braid was finished it was twisted around a pencil to create the curls and then connected to the pinback.

SQUARE PLATE BASICS

The square plate is not a traditional kumihimo tool, but a device that was developed to replicate a basic Taka Dai braid structure called Anda (plain)—a thin, flat braid similar in structure to a woven plain weave where a weft thread goes under one warp, over one, under one, etc.

The square plate has twelve slots (1–12) in the N and S sections and four slots (A–D) in the E and W sections. The numerals in the S section and letters in the E section are circled to help you differentiate the sections.

Instructions are illustrated in diagrams that replicate the square plate and show you where to place your wire or thread bundles (slots) and how to move them (arrows). Practice the braids on the plate using the same type of thread you used to practice braids on the disk and Maru Dai.

PRACTICE BRAIDS

The basic plate structure consists of two steps, both of which must be repeated to create a braid:

- One or two bundles are moved on the side of the plate (E and W), where they act as weft threads (weft = thread that goes through the warp; warp = lengthwise threads through which the weft is woven).
- The remaining bundles in N and S exchange places (S to N, N to S). In doing so, they create a new shed/pass for the weft bundles to go through.
- You can create variations of the basic braid structure depending on the number of bundles used and which bundles act as weft threads.
- No slot numbers are given for the following practice braids so you can focus on moving the threads and the correct positioning.

SIXTEEN–THREAD ANDA (PLAIN)

Set up your plate with sixteen-thread bundles in the positions indicated in the diagram for Move 1 below.

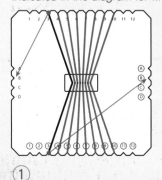

①

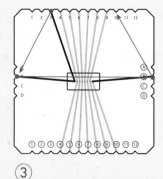

②

③

Anda point of braiding is *before* you do Step 2.

Move 1 is the initial move. After Move 1, you repeat Moves 2 and 3 until you reach the desired length.

Anda braid structure.

To create this braid, the plate was rotated 180 degrees after five repetitions, the same number of repetitions in the Zigzag Bracelet on page 113. The zigzags are more pronounced in that wire braid than in your practice (thread) braid because wire can be shaped to emphasize the slanting of the braid and thread cannot.

The point of braiding illustration (page 36) shows how the bundles in N and S rest on a diagonal line (you can see that the left side is lower than the right side). This diagonal structure gives you all sorts of interesting design possibilities.

When you work with the square plate in the standard orientation (circled numbers in S), the Anda braid will have a point on your right side. If you turn the plate 180 degrees (circled numbers in N), the point is on your left side. If you keep braiding, suddenly the braid is no longer straight but bends. Turn the plate 180 degrees, and after a while the braid will bend in the opposite direction and so on, forming a zigzag braid. The point of braiding looks the same as Anda because the structure is unchanged, but the *direction* of the diagonal line has changed, over and over again. Experiment with your own sample braid by changing the number of times you braid the Anda structure in one direction versus the other.

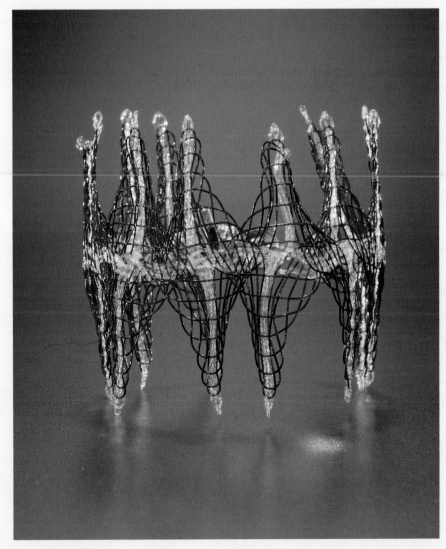

Bracelet by Leigh Morris. The bracelet was made on the square plate with wire and monofilament. It consists of two zigzag braids linked afterward to form double points.

This variation of the basic Anda braid structure is called Une (ridge). The bundles that act as the weft come from the N center slots. The remaining N/S bundles are exchanged through the center, as in Step 2 for the Anda braid (page 36), locking the weft threads in place and creating the new pass for the new weft threads.

The Raffia and Wire Necklace (page 117) uses a variation of Une that allows you to keep the same threads (or wires) in the center of the braid rather than moving around, as the basic Une does.

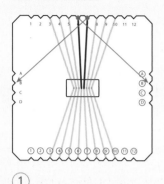

①

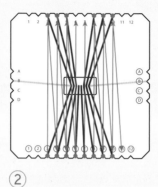

②

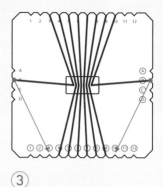

③

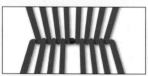

Une point of braiding.

Une braid structure.

Pendant by Maristella Ornati. Flat braid with wire, metallic thread, and beads.

SETTING UP and PREPARING TO BRAID

Setting up and braiding preparation is the same for practicing braids and creating the projects. Setting up on the disk, Maru Dai, or square plate is virtually the same, with just a few differences. And there are differences between preparing wire and preparing threads.

Takeup: When braiding with either thread or wire, there is always a certain amount of takeup (some of the length of the braiding material is used up in the interlacement)—for example, for an 8-inch (20 cm) bracelet, you measure 12 inches (30 cm) of wire. Some braid structures have more takeup than others. Your hand (how tightly you braid) also makes a difference: The more tightly you braid, the less takeup you have.

When planning a project, determine the length of the finished piece and then add 30 percent to that length for takeup. This is a general rule; you may need more or less than 30 percent, so keep notes about how much takeup you need for specific braids. The measurements provided in the projects factor in takeup.

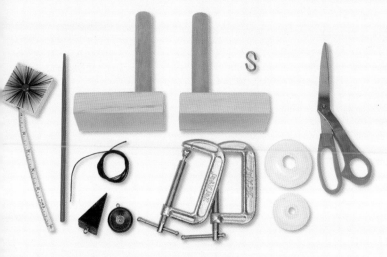

Tools needed for setup in addition to wire or thread. *Clockwise from left:* measuring tape, chopstick, warping pegs, S hook, inexpensive scissors, EZ Bobs, C-clamps, fishing weights, a few lengths of inexpensive yarn.

EZ Bobs are made of two layers of flexible plastic that are flipped open for winding wire or thread around the central core and then flipped closed. They keep threads separated and tangle free. There is enough tension between the two closed layers to keep wires and thread in place; when you need more, you simply rotate the bobbin to release it.

For the Maru Dai, in addition to the tools above left, you will need the following, *clockwise from lower left:* counterweights, bag for the counterweights, tama with leading threads (eight to twenty-four, depending on the project). The tama replace the EZ Bobs.

① Set warping pegs on a flat surface at the desired distance (i.e., if you need 12-inch wires, set the warping pegs 12 inches apart). Use C-clamps to secure them.

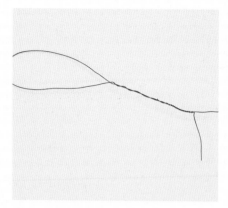

② Take the beginning of the wire from the spool and make a loop by twisting the tail.

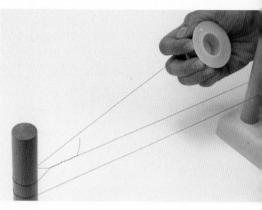

③ Place the loop around one of the pegs. Begin winding the wire by going around the opposite peg and back to the first (a complete loop). Hold the spool in your hand to prevent the wire from unraveling too fast and kinking.

④ Counting as you go, continue winding wire around the pegs; each complete loop equals two wire lengths. Once you reach the correct number of wire lengths for a bundle, tie the wires together with thread. Do not cut the wire, because you will continue winding it to make all the wire bundles required for the project at one time.

⑤ Once you measure and tie the first bundle with thread, repeat Steps 1–4 to make the next bundle and so on until all bundles needed have been measured and tied.

⑥ When all bundles have been measured and tied, make a loop around one peg and cut the wire from the spool.

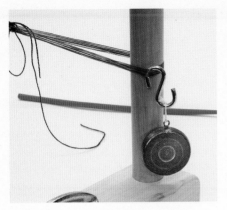

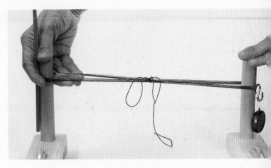

(7) On one of the warping pegs, attach the S hook and the fishing weight through all of the wires as shown.

(8) To remove the measured wire bundles from the pegs, slide the chopstick through all the tied wire bundles on the peg opposite to the peg with the S-hook and fishing weight.

(9) Remove the wire bundles from the peg at the chopstick end. Place a hand on the opposite peg to prevent the wires from jumping off.

(10) At the chopstick, twist the removed bundles tight enough so that the chopstick does not slip out. Make sure the wires are under tension by letting the fishing weight (at the opposite end) dangle.

You are now ready to set up the disk or the plate. For those projects in which you need both threads and wire, it is best to set up one or the other first rather than trying to set up both materials at once.

MEASURING THREADS FOR PROJECTS AND PRACTICE BRAIDS

The steps for measuring threads and wires are very similar. Refer to the photos and steps above. Set up the warping pegs as you would for wire (Step 1). Take the beginning of the thread and make a knotted loop (Step 2) then follow Steps 3–6 (do not twist the thread before cutting it off; knot it). Insert a chop-stick through the threads on one of the warping pegs (Step 8). Remove the thread from the warping pegs by lifting from the side where you have the chopstick (Step 9). Make a knot just under the chopstick to prevent the chopstick from sliding out. Cut the threads at the opposite end.

① Insert the wire bundles from the chopstick end through the hole of the disk or plate.

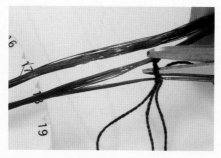

② Make sure the wire is still under tension. Use the temporary thread ties you made (Step 5 on page 40) to find your first bundle of wires. Separate that bundle by cutting the tie for that bundle.

③ Move your hand down toward the fishing weight while holding onto the bundle you have just separated. Cut that bundle from the rest of the bundles. Do not remove the fishing weight: you are separating one bundle at a time. The bundles that are not separated yet must remain tied and under tension to prevent tangling.

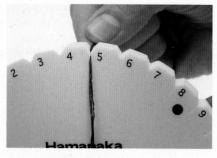

④ Place the bundle you have just separated into the appropriate slot on the disk or plate. You will need to force it through the slot to make sure that it stays in place and under tension.

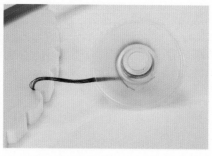

⑤ Wind the bundle you have just placed in the slot on an EZ Bob. Repeat Steps 2–5 for all the bundles of wire you have.

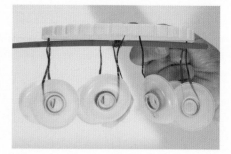

⑥ Make sure the EZ Bobs hang no more than 2 inches (5 cm) from under the plate or disk. If they are longer they will tend to tangle as you braid.

Sometimes the chopstick may get in your way. After you have set up all the bundles, you can remove it. You may want to hold the beginning of the braid with your finger under the plate as you start braiding. It will help you keep good tension and keep the braid centered in the hole.

SETTING UP THREADS ON THE DISK AND THE PLATE

For each thread bundle, follow the instructions in Steps 2 and 4 (above) for setting up wire. Because you do not need to keep threads under tension, you will not use a fishing weight and you can cut all the bundles at once. *Do not remove the temporary ties you made while measuring.*

Measure wire and threads for the Maru Dai exactly as you did for the disk and plate (pages 40–41). Setting up the Maru Dai is different, however, because you will be dealing with tama (weighted bobbins) and counterweights.

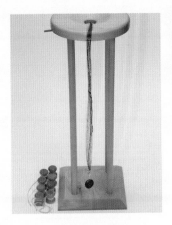

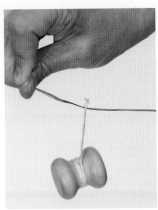

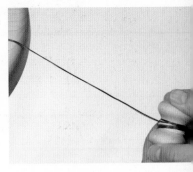

① Bring the tied wire bundles to the stand, and slide the chopstick through the central hole from the top of the mirror the same way you would with the disk (Step 1, page 42). Let the fishing weight dangle freely so that the wires remain under tension.

② Separate the wire bundles one at a time as for the disk and plate (Steps 2–4, page 42.) Insert the bundle you have just separated through the leading thread of one tama.

③ Tie the bundle and the leading thread together by twisting the wire. If you are braiding with threads, you will make a knot rather than twisting. (See sidebar on page 44 to set up the leading thread.)

④ Wind the wire bundle on the tama, maintaining an even tension and no slack. Once you are halfway between the mirror and the base, make a lark's head (half hitch) knot (see below) to prevent wire or threads from uncoiling.

⑤ After you set up all the tama, place the counterweight(s) in the bag and attach it to the all the bundles with the S hook. The counterweight should be approximately half the total weight of all the tama you wound.

MAKING A LARK'S HEAD (HALF HITCH) KNOT

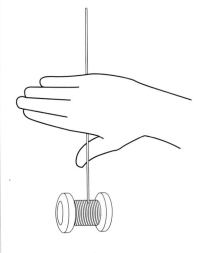

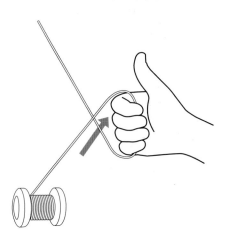

① Place your hand on the bundle just above the tama. Make sure the bundle is winding off from the underside of the tama.

② Twist your hand as shown, and slide the tama halfway through the loop you created. Pull tight.

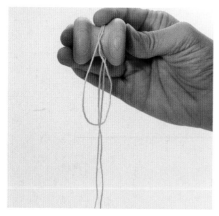

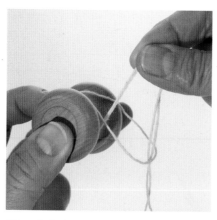

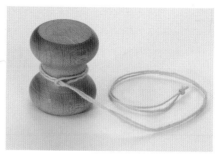

③ The tama with the leading thread in place.

① Tie the ends of an 18-inch (.5 m) length of inexpensive yarn (size 8 or 10 crochet yarn) into a knot, forming a large loop. Wrap the thread around the tama as shown.

② Pull the knotted end of the leading thread through the loop and tighten.

BRAIDING AROUND A CORE

Several disk projects use a variety of materials as cores, around which you braid. Unfortunately, there are no clear rules on how to deal with cores on the disk or the Maru Dai, so it is often a matter of experimenting and finding a solution that works for you. Here are some strategies that have worked for me in the past.

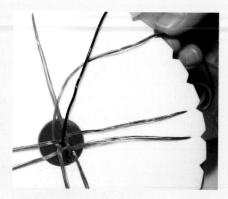

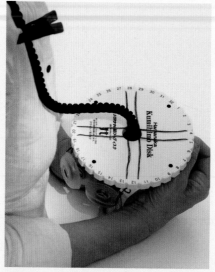

If the core is pliable (as with the Jelly Yarn used in some of the projects), simply lay the core on the disk or the Maru Dai and move the wire bundles *under* the core, as shown. To make this very clear, I turned the disk upside down in this photo so that there is no distracting writing.

If the core is large or too stiff to lay comfortably on the disk or the Maru Dai, you can clip or pin it on yourself. I know, you will look silly, but it does work: It keeps the core out of your way, and you can easily adjust the height and tension by moving the clip.

An alternative to clipping the core to yourself is to attach it to a stable object above you. Make sure that wherever you pin it, the core remains vertical relative to the disk and that you have clear visibility of the disk and the point of braiding.

FINISHING TECHNIQUES

Braided jewelry can be finished in a number of different ways. Here are four ways to finish your work, which involve different skill levels, from easy to difficult. All the finishing supplies you'll need are shown in the following three photographs.

FINISHING TOOLS AND SUPPLIES

Clockwise from bottom left: wood block, V-bench pin and clamp, three grades of sandpaper (320, 400, and 600—the higher the grade, the finer the grit), jeweler's saw with 2/0 blades, ball-peen hammer, leather mallet, wood mallet, mill file, wire cutters, flat-nose pliers, chain-nose pliers, round-nose pliers, small anvil (you can substitute a steel block).

From left: finishing spray, a variety of color pigments, E-6000 glue, permanent black marker, wax paper, two-part epoxy (Devcon two-ton brand).

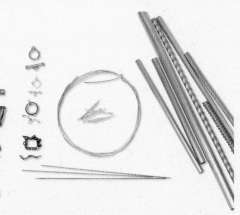

From left: a variety of end caps, end caps with clasp already attached, toggle clasps, hat pins, 18-gauge sterling silver wire, headpins, silver tubing in various diameters and textures.

FINISHING TECHNIQUE #1:
USING END CAPS WITH CLASP ALREADY ATTACHED

This is the easiest way of finishing your wire braid because it uses end caps that come with the clasps already assembled on them. All you need to do is the follow the six steps below. Sup- plies needed for this technique: Glue (E-6000 or equivalent, wax paper, toothpick).

The end caps we are using in this finishing technique have clasps already attached to them.

① Twist the loose ends on one end of the braid.

1/8"

② Trim this end of the braid by cutting excess wire, about 1/8 inch past the last braided stitch.

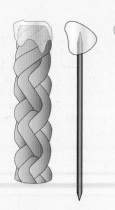

③ To attach end caps, use a toothpick to place a dab of glue (E-6000 or similar) on top of the trimmed end and around the braid. Be careful not to cover more than ¼ inch of the braid with glue.

④ Take one end cap and use a toothpick to place a dab of glue inside the cap and slide it over the glued end of the braid. Be careful not to overfill it: You need room for the braid.

⑤ Apply some pressure by pushing the end cap and braid together. Make sure that none of the glue seeps out onto the braid.

⑥ Repeat Steps 1–6 with the other end cap/clasp at the opposite end of the braid. Let the glue cure for twenty-four hours.

FINISHING TECHNIQUE #2:
USING END CAPS AND ATTACHING A SEPARATE CLASP

As you shop around for end caps, you may find some that you really like that do not come with a preassembled clasp. Or you may have a beautiful clasp but no end cap that goes with it. Don't worry. This technique shows you how to finish a braid while adding clasps to the end caps in just a few steps. Tools and supplies needed: wire cutters, two headpins, flat-nose pliers, chain-nose pliers, glue (E-6000 or equivalent), wax paper, toothpick.

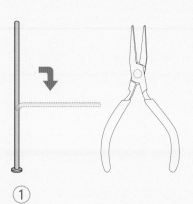

① Follow Steps 1 and 2 of Finishing Technique #1 (page 46). Take a 1-inch headpin and bend the end with the flat head to a 90-degree angle using flat-nose pliers. All you need is a small bend—¼ inch (6–7mm) maximum, from the flat head of the pin.

② Insert the headpin through the braid about ¼ inch below the end of the braid, as shown. Make sure the headpin comes out from the center of the braid's end. With your flat-nose pliers, pull gently.

③ Take your flat-nose pliers and flatten the flat head end of the headpin against the braid. The bend anchors the headpin in the braid.

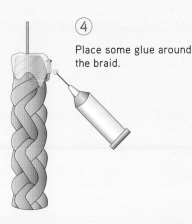

④ Place some glue around the braid.

⑤ Slide the end cap over the end of the braid, making sure the straight portion of the headpin comes out of the hole of the end cap and that the bent flat head end of the headpin is inside the end cap.

OPENING AND CLOSING JUMP RINGS

To **open a jump ring**, you need two pairs of flat-nose pliers. Hold the jump ring with one pair of pliers on each side of the cut and gently twist it open. Insert the open jump ring in the clasp. **Close the jump ring** by twisting it in the opposite direction.

⑥ Bend a loop shape in the headpin coming out of the end cap with your chain-nose pliers, as shown. Insert your clasp before fully closing the loop.

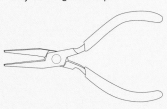

⑦ Repeat Steps 1–6 at the other end of the braid.

FINISHING TECHNIQUE #3:
MAKE YOUR OWN HOOK-AND-EYE CLASP WITH WIRE

With this technique, you will use end caps without the clasp. You will make your own hook-and-eye clasp with sterling wire. Tools and supplies needed: Two 1-inch headpins or two 2½-

inch lengths of 16- or 18-gauge sterling silver wire, flat-nose pliers, chain-nose pliers, round-nose pliers, glue (E-6000 or similar), wax paper, toothpick, mallet, and wood block.

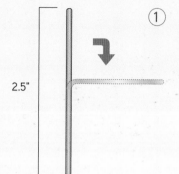

① Cut a 2½-inch length of 16- or 18-gauge wire. Use your flat-nose pliers to bend ½ inch at one end of the wire at a 90-degree angle.

2.5"

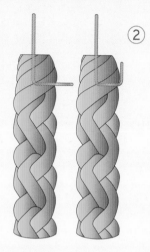

② Insert the wire through the braid about ¼ inch from the end so about 2 inches of one end of the wire comes out through the braid end and the other sticks out from the side of the braid about ¼ inch. Bend that ¼ inch so that the wire lays flat against the braid.

③ Place a dab of glue inside the end cap and slide it in place over the braid.

④ Make the hook part of the clasp. Use chain-nose pliers to bend the wire nearly 180 degrees so that the two straight sections are close to each other. You may find that tapping the sides lightly with the mallet on a wood block will help bring the two halves together.

⑤ Use the flat-nose pliers to bend half the wire back on itself, forming a hook shape. (The hook is the thickness of two wires.) Make sure the end of the bent wire is as close as possible to your end cap.

⑥ Follow Steps 1 and 2 at the opposite end of the braid. To make the eye part of the clasp, use your chain-nose pliers to bend the wire at a 90-degree angle near the end cap.

⑦ Hold that section with your chain-nose pliers and form the eye by wrapping the wire around one jaw of your round-nose pliers. Wrap the excess wire around the wire coming out of the braid under the bend.

FINISHING TECHNIQUE #4:
USING TUBING

If you have never worked with metal, you may find this method more challenging. But it is not difficult, and you may actually enjoy the design opportunities it offers. To add texture, rub the cut tube sections, before assembly, with steel wool or sandpaper. To color, use patinas or color pencils fixed with finishing spray. Tools and supplies needed: sterling silver tubing, perma-nent black marker, V-bench and clamp, jeweler's saw and 2/0 blades, mill file, two 1-inch headpins or two 2½-inch lengths of 16- or 18-gauge sterling silver wire, wire cutters, glue (E-6000 or equivalent) 2-part epoxy, wax paper, toothpick, mallet, and wood block.

① Finish the braid following Steps 1–2 on page 46. Use tubing of the correct diam-eter for your braid. The end of the braid should fit snugly inside the tube without jam-ming. If you plan to alter the shape of the tubing, pick a diameter a bit smaller than the braid.

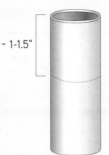

~ 1–1.5"

② Measure the correct tubing length; mark that length on the tubing with the black marker. My typical length is around 1 to 1½ inches.

③ Clamp your V-bench pin on a flat, sturdy work surface.

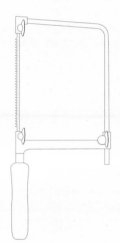

④ Insert the blade into the jeweler's saw frame so that the blade's teeth face you and are in the direction of the handle. Insert the blade in the top hole and tighten. Lean into the frame so that it buckles slightly; insert the blade in the bottom hole and tighten. Release. Pluck on the blade; if you hear a musical note, it is properly taut.

⑤ Place the tubing on the V-bench pin. Hold it firmly and make sure that the mark you made in Step 2 sits within the V. Place the saw frame at a 90-degree angle to the tube and begin to saw. Move up and down without applying too much pressure: Let the blade do the work. Cut another section in the same manner.

⑥ If you are making your own clasp or con-necting a ready-made clasp, this is the point at which you should insert a wire or a headpin into the braid, as you did in Finishing Technique #2 (Steps 2–7 on page 47) and Technique #3 (Steps 1–5 on page 48).

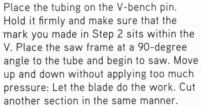

epoxy   hardener   pigment

⑦ Place a small amount of epoxy on wax paper and an equal amount of hardener next to it but not touching it. (As soon as the two parts touch, the epoxy is activated, and you don't want it acti-vated yet.) Place your color pigment next to the hardener. Use a toothpick to mix the epoxy and hardener for 1 to 2 minutes. Mix gently to avoid air bubbles. Mix the color with them.

⑧ Insert the tubing over the end of the braid. Use a toothpick to place a bit of epoxy on the top of the braid through the top of the tube. Cover the wire ends and allow some epoxy to go down the tube so it glues the tube and the braid together. Lay the glued end flat on some wax paper and let it dry. When the epoxy dries, repeat Steps 6–8 on the other end of the braid. Once dry, finish the braid by making your own hook-and-eye clasp (page 48) or by connecting a clasp (page 47).

You may sometimes find that your tubing would better fit the braid if it were not round. Some jewelry suppliers sell tubing in shapes other than round, but it is more efficient and cost effective to reshape round tubing into ovals.

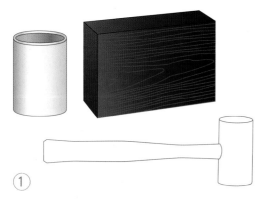

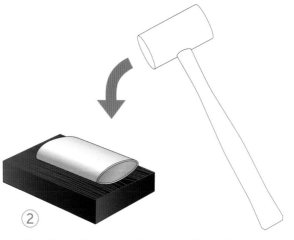

①

Once you have selected and cut the right tubing (Steps 1–5 on page 49), you can change the round tube to an oval using a wood block (or a steel block or small anvil) and a mallet.

②

Place the tubing on its side on the block. Gently tap down its length with the mallet. Be gentle. If you tap too hard or too fast, you will misshape the tubing. Check the tubing for fit regularly. Once you have the desired fit, add it to the braid (see Steps 6–8 on page 49).

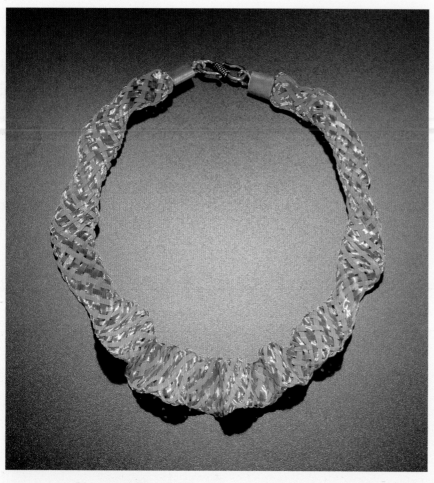

Necklace by Giovanna Imperia. Coated copper wire braided on the Maru Dai. The hollow braid (Naiki) was braided around a temporary core, which was removed afterwards. The braid was flattened and shaped by hand.

PROJECT TROUBLESHOOTING

Despite paying very close attention to the project instructions, sometimes mistakes happen. Here are some common problems you may encounter and possible fixes.

Fixing kinks and repairing breaks in wire: When you are measuring wire for a project, you may get a kink or a break. Both these problems are fixable (see below).

Wrong move or skipped move: You will know you have made a mistake when, at the end of the sequence, your point of braiding does not look like the point of braiding illustration. You will need to unbraid—that is, repeat your moves backwards until you find the error and resume braiding from that point. If you are not sure you have reached the error, keep unbraiding until you get to a recognizable point of braiding. Unbraid slowly to avoid making other mistakes.

Fixing the bends in the unbraided wire: When you unbraid wire, the unbraided section will retain the bends of the previous interlacements and will look undulating rather than straight. Some undulation can be removed by simply sliding your fingertips along that section of wire and applying some gentle pressure.

Losing your place: If you do not know or remember where you left off, look at the center of your braid. The wires that are the highest (the ones on top of all the other wires) are the wires you moved last. Now take a look at the diagrams until you find the one that shows the move that matches the wires you see on top. If you still cannot find your place, unbraid until you get to the recognizable point of braiding, then go on.

Uneven edges or bumpy braid: This is not an uncommon problem with wire, but it can also be a problem with threads. The unevenness you see is a tension problem: Sometimes the strands were pulled tighter than other times. If you notice the problem while braiding, unbraid until you reach the offending section. You can't adjust it after the braid is finished.

Point of braiding moves around the center hole: The point of braiding should always be in the center of the hole. If it moves around, it will affect tension. Pay close attention to how you move the wire: You may be pulling harder in one direction or with one hand than the other. This is not uncommon; try to adjust your movements accordingly. Also, instead of holding the disk, try holding the braid under the disk.

Tension problems at the beginning of the braid: When working on a disk or plate, it is particularly challenging to maintain an even tension at the beginning of the braid. A simple solution is to hold the beginning of the braid under the disk or the plate with your index finger. After a few rounds, it won't be necessary to continue to hold the braid.

EZ Bobs tangle while you move them: The most obvious cause of this problem is the length of the bundles exposed. Keeping your EZ Bobs at no more than 2 inches below the disk/plate will eliminate this problem.

Fixing a kink: If you have a kink in your wire, do not pull. If you look closely, you will see that the kink is nothing more than a tiny loop. To remove it, gently push the two sides of the wire toward each other. This will open up the loop. Then use your fingertips (not your nails) to gently remove any bumps in the wire.

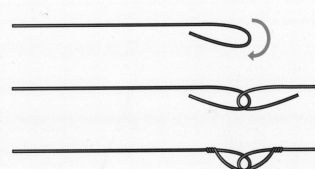

Repairing a break: Take the old and the new wire tail ends, fold them into loops, link the two loops, and twist them three or four times. When braiding through this repaired section, make sure that the ends of the wires go inside the braid so they do not stick out and scratch the skin.

Necklace by Pat Powell.

PROJECTS on the
ROUND DISK

SINGLE-BRAID BRACELET

For this project, we will use the eight-bundle structure called Yatsu Se (page 34). This is a thin, flat structure where the threads are moved around the outer edge of the disk or Maru Dai mirror instead of passing over the center. You will need to pull tight on the bundles of wire to ensure that you have a tight braid.

WHAT YOU'LL NEED

- 30-gauge (0.25 mm) coated copper wire:

  Chartreuse: 1 bundle of 10 wires per slot x 6 slots x 12 inches (30.5 cm) per wire = 20 yards (18.3 m)

  Gold: 1 bundle of 10 wires per slot x 2 slots x 12 inches (30.5 cm) per wire = 7 yards (6.4 m)

- Tools and supplies for measuring and setting up wire (page 21)

- Finishing supplies for Finishing Technique #1 (page 46)

- 2 flat end caps with closure

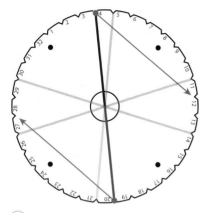

① 4 to 12
20 to 28

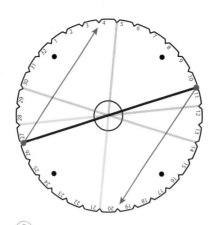

② 11 to 20
27 to 4

Reposition in the original slots.

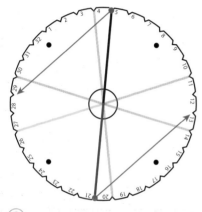

③ 5 to 29
21 to 13

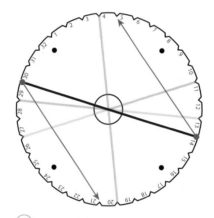

④ 14 to 5
30 to 21

Reposition in the original slots.

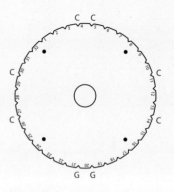

Color placement.

Point of braiding.

FINISHING

Use Finishing Technique #1 (page 46).

Detail of clasp.

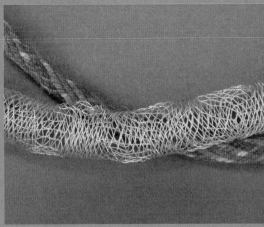

Necklace of fine silver and fiber made by Anna Hurwitz. This shows a key advantage of wire over fiber—holding shape. The silver braid was braided around a knitting needle then stretched in a way that deformed the interlacements. The needle was removed, leaving a hollow braid that will not collapse.

Bracelet by Giovanna Imperia. Although this is different braid structure from the one used in the project, it shows an easy way to create a stylish bracelet. Two braids were twisted around a heavy (10-gauge) sterling wire. The wire and the braids where glued inside a sterling tubing section. All the metal was oxidized.

THREE RINGS

For this project, you will use the eight-bundle Kongoh structure (page 28). Kongoh is a very popular structure because it is easy and fast, but it offers a large range of variations that come from color placement, materials used, and the number of bundles. You can wear the rings together in any combination or alone. The felt and button are optional; I just happen to like them. The silver band can be worn on the top or underside of the finger.

WHAT YOU'LL NEED

- 30-gauge (0.25 mm) coated copper wire:

  Purple: 1 bundle of 13 wires per slot x 6 slots x 11 inches (30 cm) = 30.8 yards (22 m)

- 28-gauge (0.32 mm) coated copper wire:

  Hot Pink: 1 bundle of 6 wires per slot x 2 slots x 11 inches (30 cm) = 3.7 yards (3.3 m)

- Tools and supplies for measuring and setting up wire (page 21)

- Finishing tools and supplies for Finishing Technique #4 (page 49)

- 1 3-inch (7.5 cm) length of curved sterling silver tubing, 4.4 mm (.17 inch) internal diameter

- 3 3 cm felt disks (optional)

- Needle and strong thread to sew felt and button to the ring (optional)

GETTING READY

To create three rings, you will work a long braid and cut it into sections. The measurements provided are based on three size 6 rings. If you want more rings or need larger sizes, simply add length. This braid has a takeup of approximately 30 percent. You will need to pull the wires tight for a nice consistent braid. Go slowly initially so you can assess how hard you should pull to achieve the desired look.

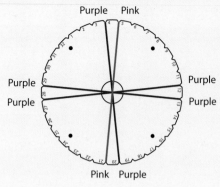

Color placement.

BRAIDING THE RINGS

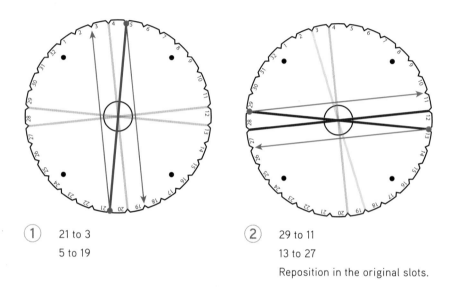

① 21 to 3
5 to 19

② 29 to 11
13 to 27
Reposition in the original slots.

Point of braiding.

FINISHING

You should have 8–9 inches (20–22 cm) of finished braid. Cut it into three equal sections and trim to fit the finger on which you will wear the rings. Saw three equal sections of the tubing (Finishing Technique #4, page 49), and file the ends to smooth the edges. If you want to add texture, sand the tubing with 320-grit sandpaper. Glue the ends of the braids into the tubing. Once the rings are fully set into the tubing, use some strong yarn to sew the button over the three felt disks and then to one of the rings.

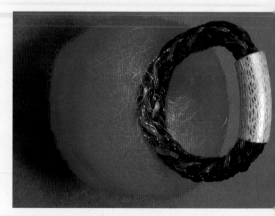

Felt disks sewn to the joined braids.

SAMPLER BRACELETS

For this project, we will use three different eight-bundle structures: Kaku Yatsu (page 31), Edo Yatsu (page 32), and Kusari Kaku Yatsu (page 30). These patterns use a technique called Tsuri Hito (thick and thin), because thin bundles of wire are mixed with thick bundles of thread. By mixing materials and bundle thicknesses in the slots, the structure is deformed and becomes more sculptural. Pull the wire tightly for an even more sculptural look.

WHAT YOU'LL NEED

- 30-gauge (0.25 mm) coated copper wire

  Gold: 1 bundle of 3 wires per slot x 4 slots x 36 inches (90 cm) per wire = 12 yards (10 m)

- Precut kumihimo silk:

  Rusty brown: 1 rope of 4 bundles, 2.8 m in length

- Tools and supplies for measuring and setting up wire (page 21)

- Finishing tools and supplies for Finishing Technique #2 (page 47)

- 6 gold-tone end caps

- 3 gold-tone clasps

- 6 1½-inch gold-tone headpins

- Masking tape (½ inch wide)

GETTING READY

You will make a single braid for all three bracelets (rather than three separate ones), which will save time. But remember to switch patterns after you reach the appropriate length for each bracelet, approximately 12 inches (30 cm) each. This is more length than you need, but it factors in possible waste when separating and finishing the braids.

BRAIDING BRACELET I

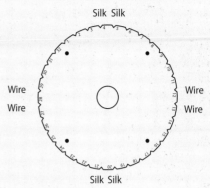

Color placement.

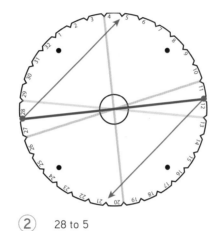

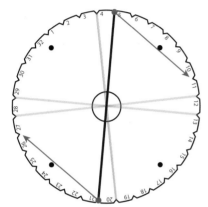

(1) 5 to 11
     21 to 27

(2) 28 to 5
     12 to 21
     Reposition: 11 to 12, 27 to 28

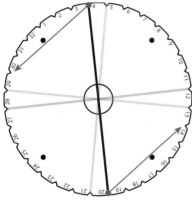

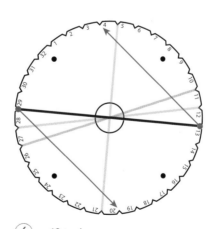

(3) 4 to 30
     20 to 14

(4) 13 to 4
     28 to 20
     Reposition: 14 to 13; 27 to 28

Point of braiding for bracelet 1.

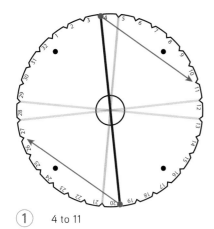

(1) 4 to 11
20 to 27

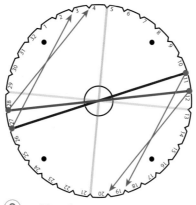

(2) 28 to 4
27 to 3
12 to 20
11 to 19

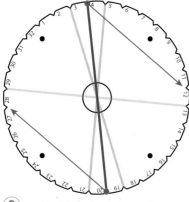

(3) 4 to 12
20 to 28
Reposition: 3 to 4, 19 to 20

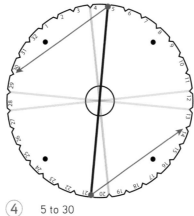

(4) 5 to 30
21 to 14

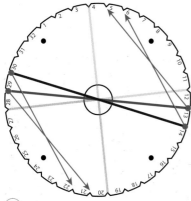

(5) 13 to 5
14 to 6
29 to 21
30 to 22

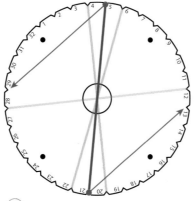

(6) 5 to 29
21 to 13
Reposition: 6 to 5, 22 to 21

+ TIP

When the braid for bracelet 2 is executed on the Maru Dai, Steps 2 and 5 require you to move four tama while twisting them, always in the same direction.

Point of braiding for bracelet 2.

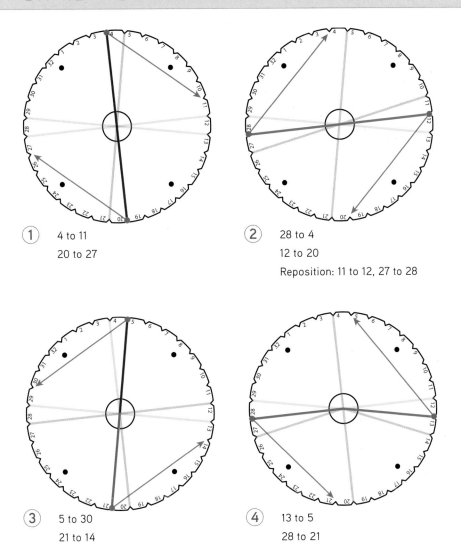

① 4 to 11
20 to 27

② 28 to 4
12 to 20
Reposition: 11 to 12, 27 to 28

③ 5 to 30
21 to 14

④ 13 to 5
28 to 21
Reposition: 14 to 13, 27 to 28

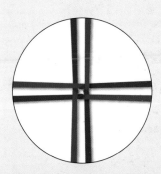

Point of braiding for bracelet 3.

FINISHING

Once the braid length for all three bracelets is completed, wrap masking tape around the braid in between patterns to prevent threads from unraveling. Cut the braid in the middle of the tape. If the tape will show under the end cap, trim the braid some, but leave at least ¼ inch of taped end. With the three braids now separated, measure them to fit the wrist. (Remember to factor in the length of the clasp!) If too long, wrap tape at the appropriate length and cut. Use Finishing Technique #2 (page 47) to attach the end caps.

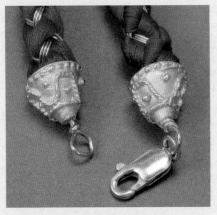

Clasp attached to end of braid.

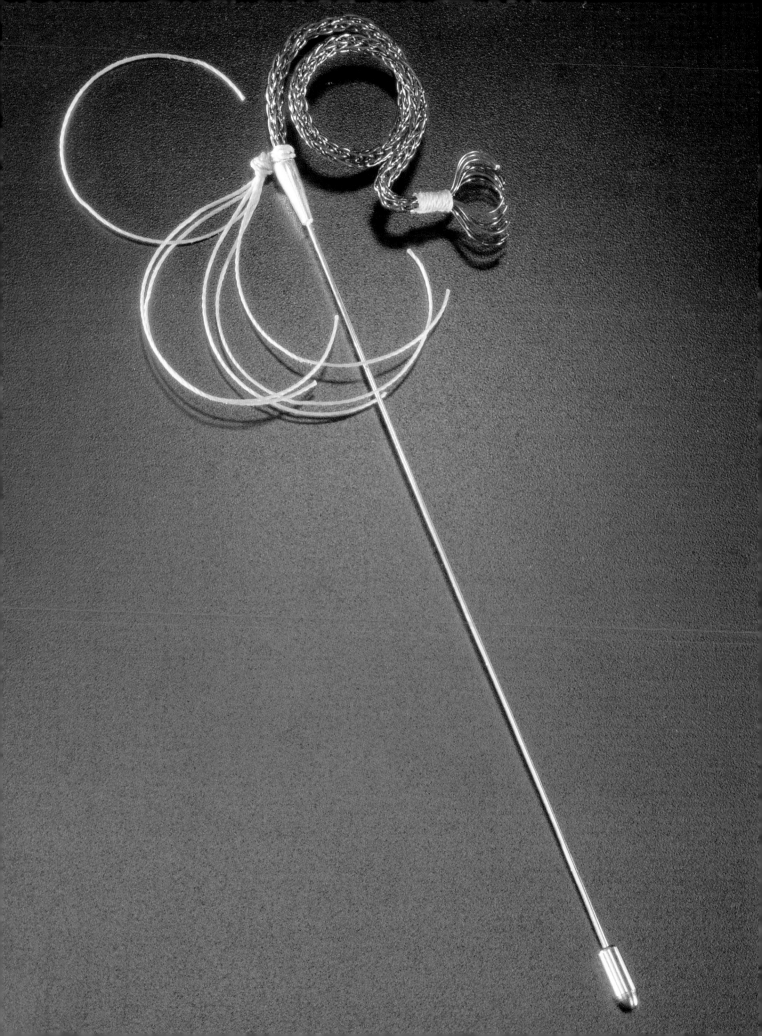

CURLY STICK PIN

PROJECT BY **PAT POWELL**

For this project, you will use a sixteen-bundle structure called Maru Genji (page 30). Even when executed with silk, this braid requires tightening, so make sure you pull hard on your wires, which give stability to the curly portion of the pin. Because this pin calls for 26-gauge (0.40mm) wire, it is possible to shape the end of the braid in a curved wire tassel.

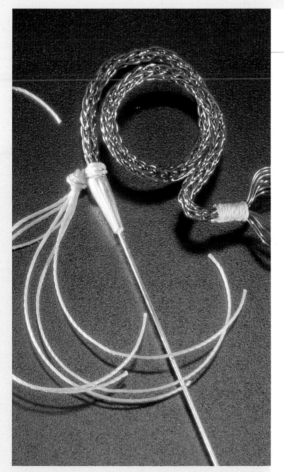

WHAT YOU'LL NEED

- 26-gauge (0.40 mm) coated copper wire:

  Magenta: 1 wire per slot x 4 slots x 32 inches (81 cm) per wire = 3.5 yards (3.2 m)

  Blue: 1 wire per slot x 4 slots x 32 inches (81 cm) per wire = 3.5 yards (3.2 m)

- You will fold the wires in half around a chopstick, so you will end up with 16 wires to place in the appropriate 16 slots (see color placement diagram). You will need 16 EZ Bobs.

- Tools and supplies for measuring and setting up wire (page 21)

- Finishing tools for Finishing Technique #2 (page 47)

- 1 additional chopstick

- 1 long stick pin or hat pin

- 1 end cap

- 1 yard C-Lon yarn, chartreuse

GETTING READY

Note that you will fold your wires in half around a chopstick so you will place 16 wires in the appropriate slots. To keep the chopstick in place, twist the wires.

BRAIDING THE STICK PIN

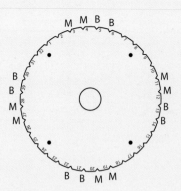

Color placement.

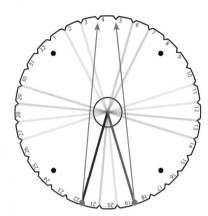

① Move the threads in the North position sideways so that slots 4 and 5 are empty.

22 to 4; 19 to 5

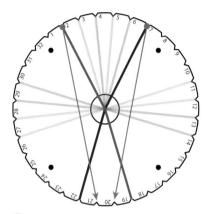

② Move the threads in the South position sideways so that slots 20 and 21 are empty.

2 to 21; 7 to 20

+ TIP

Do not be too concerned about colors. After the first sequence, the two colors will start trading places. It takes four sequences before colors return to their original positions.

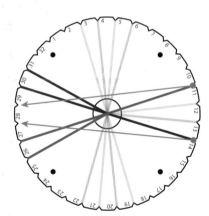

③ Move the threads in the West position sideways so that slots 28 and 29 are empty.

11 to 29; 14 to 28

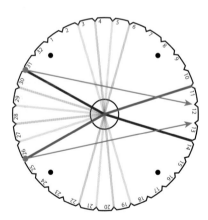

④ Move the threads in the East position sideways so that slots 12 and 13 are empty.

31 to 12; 26 to 13

Point of braiding.

FINISHING

Remove the chopstick. Use the C-Lon yarn to do a decorative wrap around the beginning of the braid (where you twisted the wire). Cut the wire. Because the wire was around the chopstick, it will be bent into a loop. Fan out the ends, as in the photo. Follow directions in Finishing Technique #2 to insert the hatpin in the braid and connect the end cap. Then curve the braid and add a tassel of C-Lon yarn, as in the photo.

Point at which stick pin, braid, and tassel converge.

Bracelet by Giovanna Imperia. A small metal braid was created first and then braided together with hand-dyed silk.

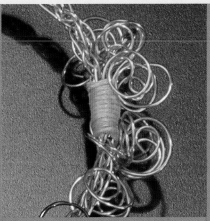

Bracelets by Pat Powell. These bracelets (in 20-gauge coated copper wire) were finished with C-Lon threads like the Curly Stick Pin. Rather than attempting to hide the thick wire ends, which would have resulted in a very thick and unattractive wrapping, Pat curved the ends in a random pattern over a much thinner wrapping. The curling was done by hand around a pencil.

LACY BRACELET

This braid is a compound braid that combines Edo Yatsu (page 32) and Maru Genji (page 30). There are two sets of moves: (1) Wires move around the edge of the disk (Edo Yatsu) and (2) bundle pairs are exchanged over the center (Genji). By using a slightly stiffer wire (28-gauge) and not pulling too hard, the braid pattern will be open and lacy.

WHAT YOU'LL NEED

- 28-gauge (0.32 mm) coated copper wire:

  Dark green: 1 bundle of 4 wires per slot x 16 slots x 12 inches (30.5 cm) per wire = 21 yards (19.4 m)

- Tools and supplies for measuring and setting up wire (page 21)

- Finishing supplies for Finishing Technique #1 (page 46)

- 2 flat (10 mm) end caps with closure

- Wood block

- Mallet

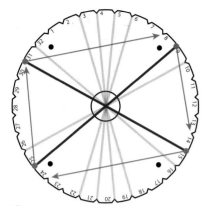

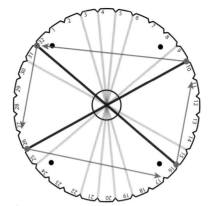

(1) 31 to 8
     9 to 14
     15 to 24
     25 to 31
     Reposition in the original slots.

(2) 32 to 27
     26 to 17
     16 to 11
     10 to 32
     Reposition in the original slots.

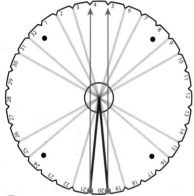

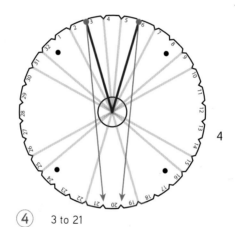

4

(3) Move 3 and 4 one slot over.
     Move 5 and 6 one slot over.
     21 to 4
     20 to 5

(4) 3 to 21
     6 to 20

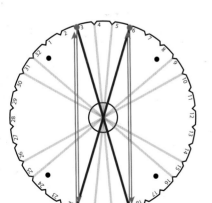

(5) 22 to 3
     3 to 22
     19 to 6
     6 to 19

+ TIP

Do not tighten the threads as you move them. This will yield a more open and lacey braid.

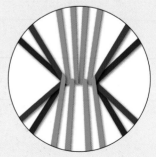

Point of braiding.

FINISHING

To emphasize the flatness of the braid, tap it gently with a mallet on a wood block before attaching the end caps. Use Finishing Technique #1 (page 46).

End caps attached to braid.

Bracelet by Carole McAllister. Although this is not the same structure used for the Lacy Bracelet, it is a very interesting and creative interpretation of a open lacy structure that works only because it is done in wire. Carole used a traditional bobbin lace technique on the Maru Dai.

Necklace by Carole MacAllister. This necklace was braided with coated copper wire. Carole was able to create the lacy effect by loosely interlacing three braids.

BLACK + COPPER CUFF

For this project we will use an eight-bundle braid called Edo Yatsu (page 32). It is a hollow braid, making it very suitable for braiding around a core (page 44). This project is classified Intermediate not because the structure is difficult but because you have to deal with a flat strip of copper as your core. The copper strip is seen through the braid because you use fewer wire ends per slot.

WHAT YOU'LL NEED

- 30-gauge (0.25 mm) coated copper wire:

  Black: 1 bundle of 7 wires per slot x 8 slots x 15 inches (35.6 cm) per wire = 23 yards (21 m)

- Tools and supplies for measuring and setting up wire (page 21)

- Finishing tools for Finishing Technique #4 (page 49)

- 1 6-inch long (15 cm), ½-inch-wide (1.3 cm), 18-gauge (1.02 mm) flat copper strip

- 1 2-inch (5 cm) length of sterling silver tubing, 10.55 mm (.42 inch) diameter (to be cut into two 1-inch lengths)

GETTING READY

The copper strip is the core, and you'll braid around it, but it has sharp corners that may cut into the wire, so round them with the mill file. Sand both sides of the strip, keeping the finish consistent. To protect the bright copper finish, spray with finishing spray. Initially, it may be difficult to keep the core in place. Don't worry. Braid slowly without pulling on the wire. After three to four sequences, the wire will start to grip the strip (core). It helps to push the strip down into the braid (or pull it from underneath) after each sequence. Once the wire grips the strip, braiding will be easy and fast.

BRAIDING THE RINGS

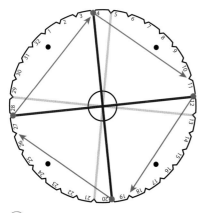

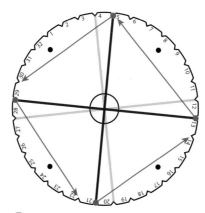

Point of braiding.

① 4 to 11
12 to 19
20 to 27
28 to 4
Reposition in the original slots.

② 5 to 30
29 to 22
21 to 14
13 to 4
Reposition in the original slots.

Braid for about ¾ inch; do not pull tight. (This is the beginning of the braid, which will be trimmed and placed inside the end cap.) Place the strip in the hole at the center of the braid, pushing a bit to allow the braid to grab it. It's not possible to push the strip through the entire braid, so don't force it. Your objective is to have the strip reasonably stable and in a vertical position relative to the disk. As you braid around it, the wire will grab the strip and it will become increasingly stable. Keep your braiding loose so the copper is quite visible through the wire. Braid over the entire strip plus ¾ inch, take the braid off the disk, and finish.

FINISHING

Use Finishing Technique #4 (page 49). Because we are using a flat strip as the core, the resulting cuff is flat, so the tubing has to be flattened to fit.

Once the epoxy is fully cured, you can bend the braid to form it into a cuff. The copper strip is soft enough that you should be able to bend it with your hands. If you cannot, find something 8 to 9 inches in diameter such as a baseball bat or PVC pipe, place the strip on it, and start tapping with a mallet until is fully bent (see below).

Detail of the cuff showing the silver tubing and the colored epoxy.

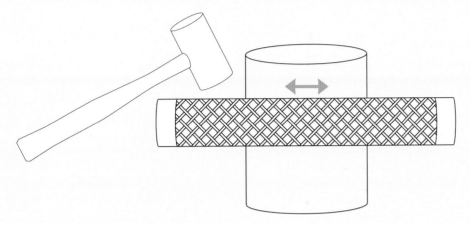

How to bend the cuff: Tap from the center out. Go from one side to the other. Periodically stop and try on the cuff to make sure it fits properly.

This is a very interesting study of materials and cores by Shirley Berlin. The top three braids are the same hollow structure. The copper and red bracelets were braided around different-sized knitting needles, removed afterward. The three-color bracelet was braided with vintage telephone wire with no cores. The purple and white necklace is a different structure where Shirley experimented with shifting from no core to increasing sizes of cores.

TWISTED NECKLACE
WITH **BEADS**

For this project, you will use a compound braid. The twelve white bundles, positioned in S and N, form the Naiki pattern (page 33), and the four (black) bundles, positioned in E and W, form the Kongoh structure (page 28). The combination of these two structures creates a flat braid that will spiral onto itself, and you will need extra wire length for the takeup of the spiraling.

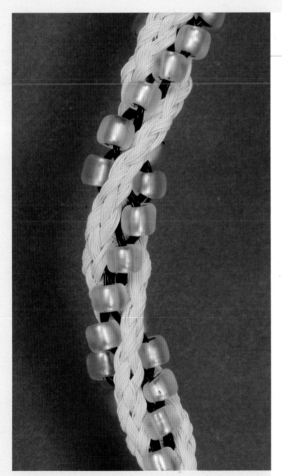

WHAT YOU'LL NEED

- 34-gauge (0.16 mm) coated copper wire:

  White: 1 bundle of 12 wires per slot x 12 slots x 1 yard (0.9 m) per wire = 144 yards (131 m)

- 28-gauge (0.32 mm) coated copper wire:

  Black: 1 bundle of 4 wires per slot x 4 slots x 1 yard (0.9 m) per wire = 16 yards (14.5 m)

- 230 size 6 seed beads (roughly 15 g):

  Color: F1 by Miyuki of Japan

- Tools and supplies for measuring and setting up wire (page 21)

- Finishing tools and supplies for Finishing Technique #2 (page 47)

- 2 end caps

- 1 toggle clasp

STRINGING THE BEADS

After you set up all the wire bundles in the proper slots, string approximately fifty-seven beads on each of the four black bundles, placing only two beads at a time on the active bundles (the ones you are moving). Braid the first inch or so without beads (this part will be hidden in the end cap), and then start adding beads. Make sure to place the beads on the *outside* of the braid. When you move the white wires, make sure the beads remain under them. Tug on the black wires after each Naiki sequence. Don't be alarmed if your braid doesn't seem to spiral as you work; wire has a tendency to keep the braid straight. You will be able to make adjustments afterward.

Color placement.

BRAIDING THE NECKLACE

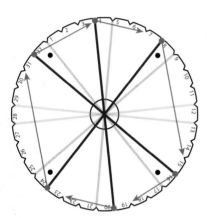

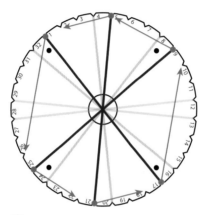

(1) 4 to 7
    8 to 15
    16 to 19
    20 to 23
    24 to 31
    32 to 4
    Reposition in the original slots.

(2) 5 to 2
    1 to 26
    25 to 22
    21 to 18
    17 to 10
    9 to 5
    Reposition in the original slots.

Point of braiding.

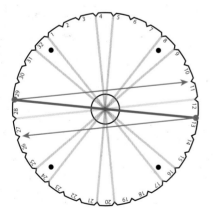

(3) 13 to 27
    29 to 11
    Reposition in the original slots.

This point of braiding shows how the beads "sit" under the wires just moved.

FINISHING

Once you have finished the braid, you may need to twist it some to emphasize the spiraling effect. Use Finishing Technique #2 (page 47).

End caps attached to braid.

Necklace by Sandy Jassett. Sandy strung the beads on thread making sure she spaced the drops consistently. She then braided a flat braid (Hira Kara) making sure that three beads stayed on one edge of the braid and the remaining beads (with drop) stayed on the other edge. She then shaped the finished braid with the drops on the outer edge of the braid.

Necklace by Carol MacAllister. Carol mixes various fibers, uncoated copper wire, and beads in this very interesting necklace. The choice of same-tone materials creates a very subtle texture variation.

DOUBLE-STRAND NECKLACE

WITH **LARGE FELT BEADS**

For this project you will use an eight-bundle square structure called Kaku Yatsu (page 31). You will (1) string felt beads on Jelly Yarn and (2) braid the wire using the Jelly Yarn as a core (page 44). Note that only roughly half of the braid uses the Jelly Yarn and felt beads.

WHAT YOU'LL NEED

- 32-gauge (0.20 mm) coated copper wire:

  Silver blue: 1 bundle of 15 wires per slot x 8 slots x 72 inches (1.8 m) per wire = 240 yards (20 m)

- Jelly Yarn (fine gauge):

  Black: 3 yards (2.7 m)

- Tools and supplies for measuring and setting up wire (page 21)

- Finishing tools and supplies for Finishing Technique #3 (page 48)

- 26 3-inch (7.6 cm) diameter felt beads (balls). Set one aside; you will need it for the closure.

- Long tapestry needle

- 2 end caps

STRINGING THE FELT BEADS

Using the large tapestry needle, pierce the felt beads through their centers and string them on the Jelly Yarn following the diagram below. Knot the Jelly Yarn between each bead to keep them from slipping off. When going back into the bead, make sure you go through the same hole you just created. Once you string all the felt beads, your finished length should be approximately 48 inches. Jelly Yarn, which is made out of vinyl, is a bit stretchy, so be careful not to pull too hard as you go in and out of the felt beads and when you braid around it.

Point of braiding.

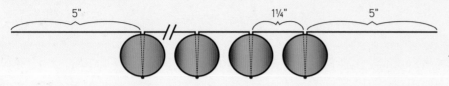

+ **TIP**

Make sure you braid around the Jelly Yarn—always move the wires under the Jelly Yarn, never over it.

BRAIDING THE NECKLACE

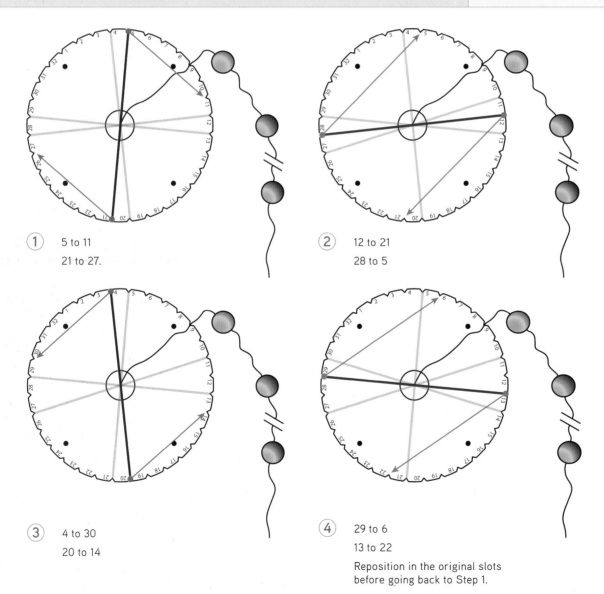

① 5 to 11
21 to 27.

② 12 to 21
28 to 5

③ 4 to 30
20 to 14

④ 29 to 6
13 to 22

Reposition in the original slots before going back to Step 1.

Once you set up the wire in the appropriate slots, do a couple of sequences without the Jelly Yarn core. Next, place one of the Jelly Yarn tails across the point of braiding, leaving 4½ inches of that tail outside of the braid. Start braiding again. Pull very tightly after each sequence so the Jelly Yarn core is fully locked inside the braid. This is an important step, as this braid structure is not hollow.

When you reach a ball, push it through the center hole of the disk to one side of the braid. Make sure you push all the balls from the same side of the braid. When you have pushed the last felt bead through the hole, braid around the Jelly Yarn for about ½ inch. Leave the remaining tail outside of the braid. Continue braiding without the core. You should have approximately 21 inches of beadless braid.

FINISHING

You will use Finishing Technique #3, but you will not make your clasp out of wire. You will use the tails of Jelly Yarn instead.

Remove the completed braid from the disk and twist the ends as usual. Fold the braid at the point where the tail of the Jelly Yarn sticks out of the braid and twist the two sections of the braid together. You do not need to cut the braid; just bend it tightly. If needed, use flat-nose pliers to press the bent braid together.

Make a loop with one of the tails by sliding the end of the Jelly Yarn tail through the braid. Apply a bit of glue and slide it into the end cap, making sure the loop comes out of the end cap's top hole.

Apply a bit of glue on the other end of the braid and slide the other end cap onto it. Make sure the tail comes out of the top hole. Thread the felt bead you set aside onto the Jelly Yarn tail and secure with a knot.

End caps attached to braid; closure (clasp).

Lariat, by Giovanna Imperia. This neck piece consists of a very thin uncoated copper wire braid. Felt balls hang from the Jelly Yarn braid.

FRESHWATER PEARLS NECKLACE

For this project you will use the hollow Naiki braid (page 33) worked around a core. Because the core is large, you may find it easier to suspend it as you work (page 44) rather than lay it on the top of the disk. The beauty of this braid comes from the loose interlacement, which allows the cord core underneath to show. It is important to select a good quality cord. Check upholstery stores or good fabric stores.

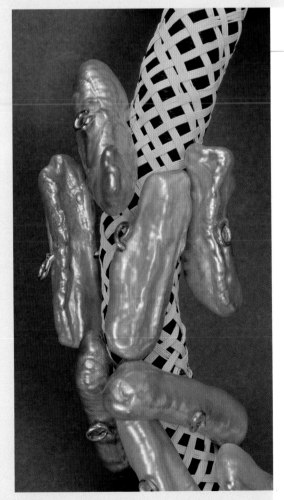

WHAT YOU'LL NEED

- 34-gauge (0.127 mm) coated copper wire:

  Matte white: 1 bundle of 5 wires per slot x 16 slots x 36 inches (90 cm) per wire = 80 yards (72 m)

- 20-gauge sterling silver wire (for stringing pearls):

  15-inch (37 cm) length

- Black upholstery cording:

  9mm diameter; 18-inch length

- 14 long freshwater pearls (center drill, stick shape), pearl gray

- One 2-inch (5 cm) length of sterling silver tubing, 11 mm (.43 inch) diameter

- Toggle clasp (silver color)

- Tools and supplies for measuring and setting up wire (page 21)

- Finishing tools for Finishing Technique #4 (page 49)

- Long tapestry needle

- Pearl reamer (optional)

GETTING READY

To achieve the open look of this braid, we will use fewer wire ends per slot and will also not pull the wire hard around the core. You may want to add a small weight under the disk as the braid is formed because the weight will pull the braid down and stretch the interlacements.

BRAIDING THE NECKLACE

+ TIP

Do not be too concerned about colors. After the first sequence, the two colors will start trading places. It takes four sequences before colors return to their original positions.

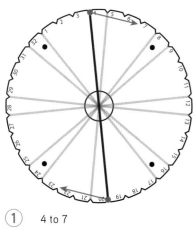

①   4 to 7
        20 to 23

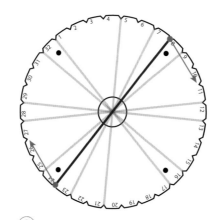

②   8 to 11
        24 to 27

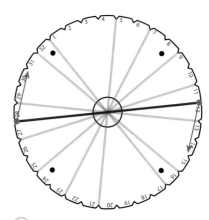

③   12 to 15
        28 to 31

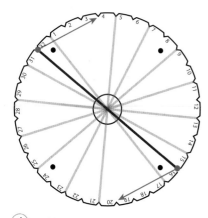

④   32 to 4
        16 to 20

Reposition in the original slots:
7 to 8; 11 to 12; 15 to 16; 23 to 24; 27 to 28; 31 to 32.

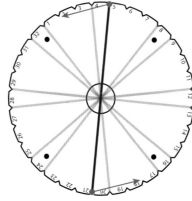

⑤   21 to 18
        5 to 2

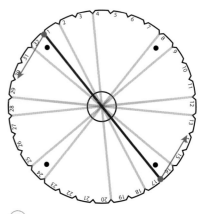

⑥   17 to 14
        1 to 30

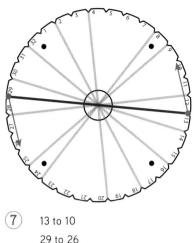

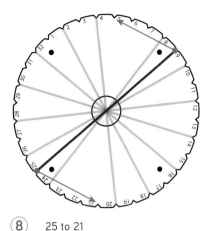

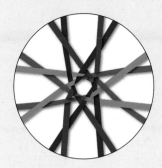

Point of braiding.

⑦   13 to 10
      29 to 26

⑧   25 to 21
      9 to 5

Reposition in the original slots:
10 to 9; 14 to 13; 18 to 17; 26 to
25; 30 to 29; 2 to 1.

FINISHING

Finish with Finishing Technique #4 (page 49). Wait until the epoxy is fully cured before attaching the pearls. You may also want to add some texture to the silver tubing by rubbing it with sandpaper before you assemble the tubing and the braid.

ADDING THE PEARLS

Make sure the pearls are in the center of the necklace. Cut the sterling silver wire into seven 1- to 1½-inch lengths. Using the needle-nose pliers, make a small loop at one end of the wire and slide on one pearl. (If the drilled hole is too small, enlarge it with a pearl reamer.) Use the tapestry needle to create a passage through the core. Insert the wire in the passage you just created and insert another pearl on it. Make a loop to secure the pearl and cut off the excess wire. Repeat for all the pearls.

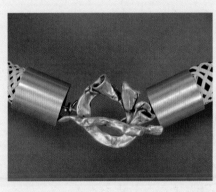

Tubing attached to braid and closure (clasp).

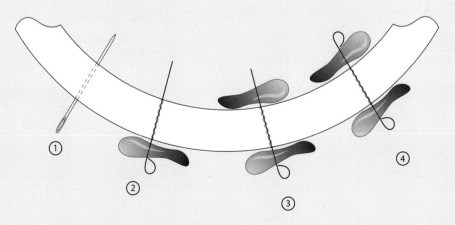

①   ②   ③   ④

TWO-COLOR BRACELET

For this project, we will use the traditional sixteen-bundle structure called Kata Sa-sanami. Be extra careful with the stainless steel wire, as it is much springier than coated copper wire. You also need to pull a bit more when moving the steel, as it tends to remain more open than the copper wire.

WHAT YOU'LL NEED

- 36-gauge (0.13 mm) coated copper wire:

  Dark olive: 1 bundle of 20 wires per slot x 8 slots x 12 inches (30 cm) per wire = 53 yards (48 m)

- 36 gauge (0.13 mm) stainless steel wire:

  1 bundle of 20 wires per slot x 8 slots x 12 inches (30 cm) per wire = 53 yards (48 m)

- Tools and supplies for measuring and setting up wire (page 21)

- Finishing tools and supplies for Finishing Technique #4 (page 49)

- 2-inch length of sterling silver tubing, 5mm (.20 inch) diameter

- 2 1½-inch silver headpins

- Silver clasp of your choice

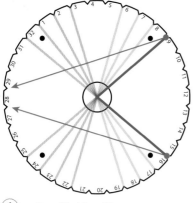

(1) 9 to 29; 16 to 28

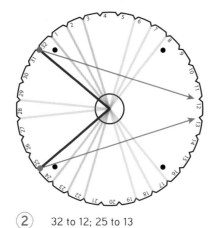

(2) 32 to 12; 25 to 13

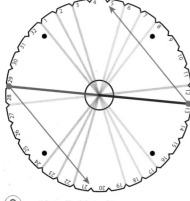

(3) 13 to 5; 29 to 21

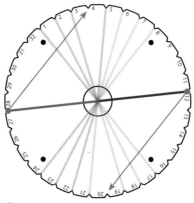

(4) 28 to 4; 12 to 20

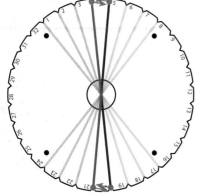

(5) Exchange: 4 to 5 and 5 to 4; 21 to 20 and 20 to 21

(5) 24 to 1; 1 to 24

23 to 2; 2 to 23

22 to 3; 3 to 22

21 to 4; 4 to 21

17 to 8; 8 to 17

18 to 7; 7 to 18

19 to 6; 6 to 19

20 to 5; 5 to 20

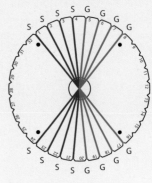

Color placement diagram.

Point of braiding.

FINISHING

Use Finishing Technique #4 (page 49). Because this is a flat braid, you have to flatten the tubing for a better fit. You can emphasize the central ridge of the braid by gently pushing the two edges toward each other.

Tubing end caps attached to braid and closure (clasp).

Necklace by Lidia Musetti. This is a good example of how very fine wire will yield a tight structure similar to threads. It is also interesting to see how Lidia finished the braid: She created two spirals between three focal beads, a simple but effective design.

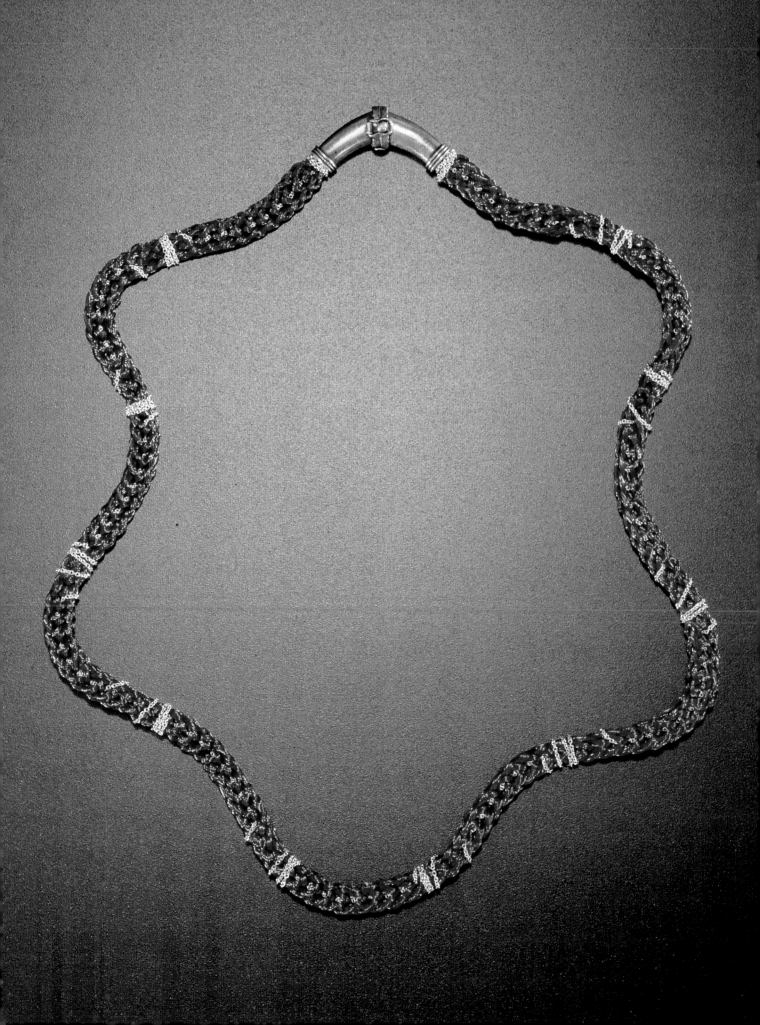

IN-AND-OUT NECKLACE

For this project, you will use the twelve-bundle structure Yatsu Se (page 34), which you will braid around a silver chain. Because this is a flat braid, the wire will not hide the chain, which will appear intermittently in the center of the braid.

WHAT YOU'LL NEED

- 32-gauge (0.20 mm) coated copper wire:

  Burnt brown: 1 bundle of 10 wires per slot x 12 slots x 36 inches (90 cm) per wire = 120 yards (109 m)

- 5 feet (1.5 m) very small sterling chain (between .5 and 1 mm)

- Tools and supplies for measuring and setting up wire (page 21)

- Finishing supplies for Finishing Technique #1 (page 46)

- Extra EZ Bob for the chain

- Hill Tribes silver bent tube clasp

GETTING READY

Before you start, wind most of the chain length on an EZ Bob and tie one end of it together with the wire. Lay the chain on the top of the disk with the EZ Bob hanging off the edge.

BRAIDING THE NECKLACE

Point of braiding.

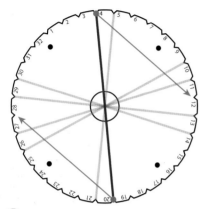

① Move two of the threads in the East and West positions sideways so that slots 12 and 28 are empty.

4 to 12; 20 to 28

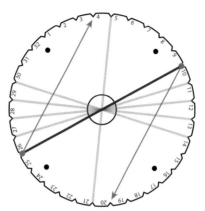

② 26 to 4; 10 to 20

+ **TIP**

Pull tight on the wire so that you will have a fairly stiff braid, which will be easier to shape.

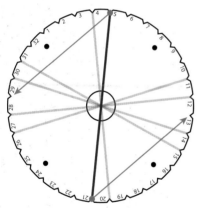

③ Move the threads in the E and W position sideways so that slots 13 and 29 are empty.

21 to 13; 5 to 29

④ 31 to 21; 15 to 5

Every 2½ inches (6.4 cm), move the chain from the top of the disk to underneath it. Then braid three to four sequences without the chain. Wind the chain three or four times around this section of the braid and then move it back on the top of the disk. Repeat ten times.

FINISHING

Use Finishing Technique #1 (page 46). Allow the glue to cure and then shape the braid. Because I used a curved clasp, I chose to repeat the same undulation in the braid, but you can choose a different pattern.

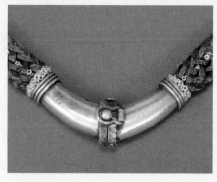

End caps attached to braid and closure (clasp).

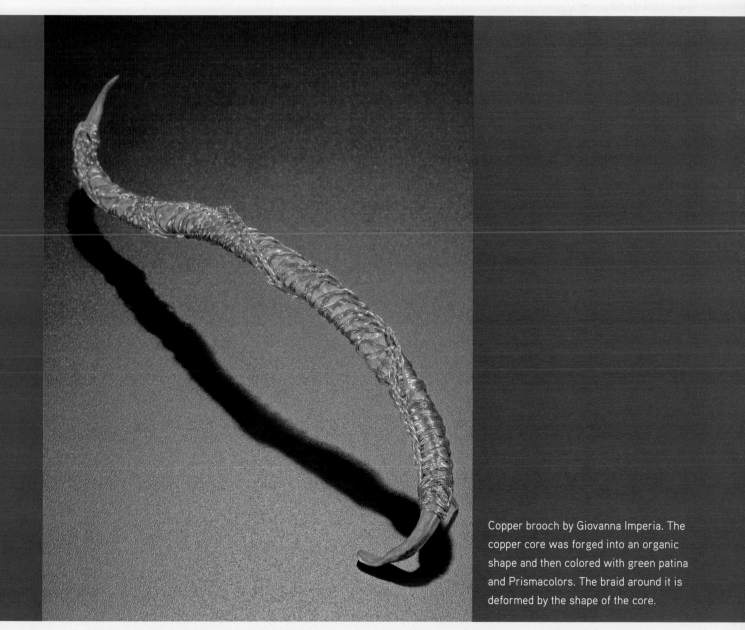

Copper brooch by Giovanna Imperia. The copper core was forged into an organic shape and then colored with green patina and Prismacolors. The braid around it is deformed by the shape of the core.

INTERTWINED BRAIDS BRACELET

PROJECT BY **LIDIA MUSETTI**

The structure used in this project is similar to Hira Nami Yatsu (page 34), but it is executed with twenty-four bundles rather than eight. Pay close attention to the initial color placement. Colors move with every step, which creates very attractive bands of color throughout the braid.

The interesting feature of this project is that it uses extremely fine wire and therefore looks like it was braided with silk.

WHAT YOU'LL NEED

- 36-gauge (0.12 mm) coated copper wire:

  Green: 1 bundle of 10 wires per slot x 8 slots x 63 inches (1.6 m) per wire = 17.5 yards (16 m)

  Silver: 1 bundle of 10 wires per slot x 8 slots x 63 inches (1.6 m) per wire = 17.5 yards (16 m)

  Natural or bare: 1 bundle of 10 wires per slot x 8 slots x 63 inches (1.6 m) per wire = 17.5 yards (16 m)

- Tools and supplies for measuring and setting up wire (page 21)

- Finishing supplies for Finishing Technique #1 (page 46)

- End caps with clasp

GETTING READY

Before you start, wind most of the chain length on an EZ Bob and tie one end of it together with the wire. Lay the chain on the top of the disk with the EZ Bob hanging off the edge.

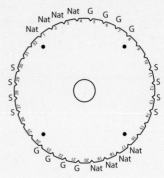

Color placement.

BRAIDING THE BRACELET

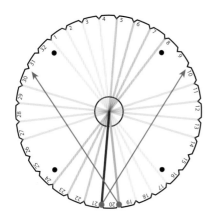

①   20 to 31
       21 to 10

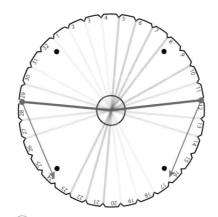

②   22 to 21; 23 to 22; 24 to 23
       19 to 20; 18 to 19; 17 to 18
       29 to 24; 12 to 17

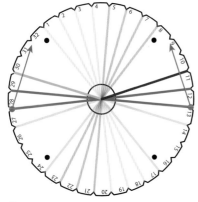

③   30 to 29; 31 to 30
       11 to 12; 10 to 11
       28 to 32; 13 to 9

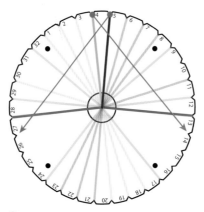

④   27 to 28; 14 to 13
       5 to 27; 4 to 14

Point of braiding.

FINISHING

Once the braid is completed, cut it in half. Glue all the ends to prevent it from unraveling. Once dry, twist the two sections, making sure they remain flat. Add the end caps with clasp as in Finishing Technique #1 (page 46).

End caps attached to braid and closure (clasp).

BRAIDED BEADS NECKLACE

For this project you will use the eight-bundle Edo Yatsu structure (page 32). The biggest challenge is to braid around the large round beads because the beads are big and slippery and the wire is also slippery. Accept a certain amount of randomness as a design element. If that bothers you, substitute the large round beads with smaller beads or different shapes, such as ovals, ridged, or square, which are less likely to slip or move than round beads.

WHAT YOU'LL NEED

- 32-gauge (0.20 mm) coated copper wire:

  Lemon: 1 bundle of 10 wires per slot x 4 slots x 36 inches (90 cm) per wire = 40 yards (36 m)

  Matte yellow: 1 bundle of 10 wires per slot x 4 slots x 36 inches (90 cm) per wire = 40 yards (36 m)

- 6 17mm vintage acrylic beads (or similar size; look for interesting finishes, as the beads will show through the braid)

- 30 inches (75 cm) rattail or other thick cord, any color (this will be completely covered by the braid)

- Tools and supplies for measuring and setting up wire (page 21)

- Finishing supplies for Finishing Technique #1 (page 46)

- End caps with clasp

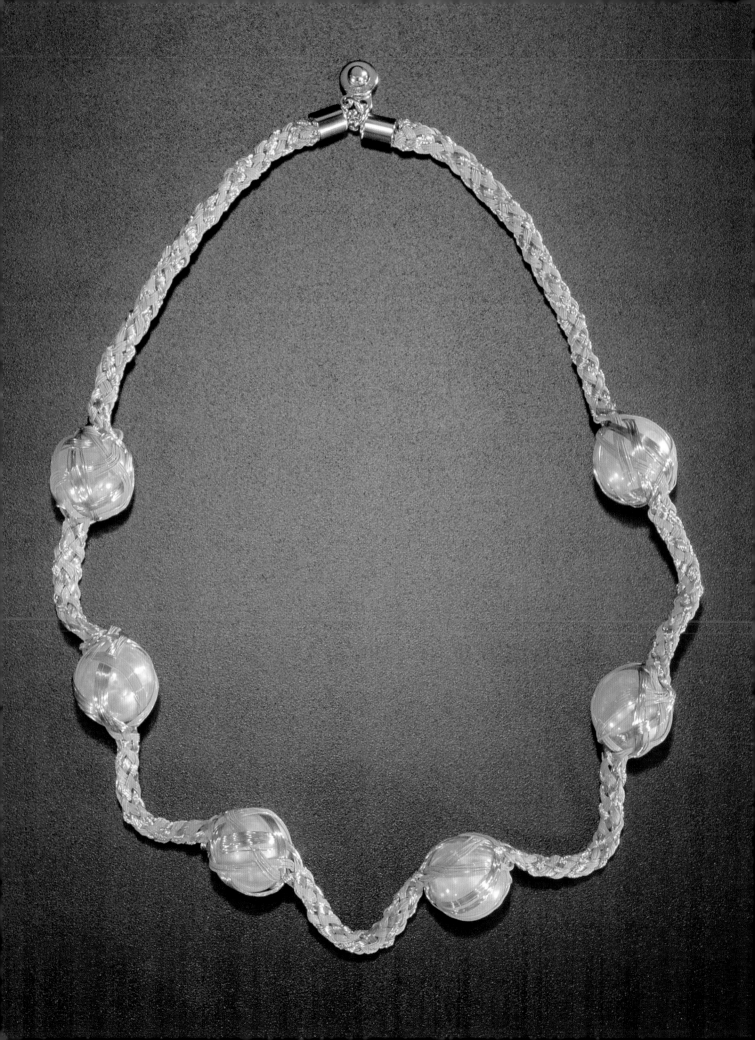

STRINGING THE BEADS

To help manage the beads, string them on rattail or another thick cord. Make a knot before and after each bead. This will prevent the beads from moving and slipping as you braid around them. Follow this diagram:

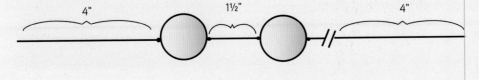

Point of braiding.

+ **TIP**

Select a cord that can go easily through the beads' holes but is thick enough to require only one knot before and after each bead.

BRAIDING THE NECKLACE

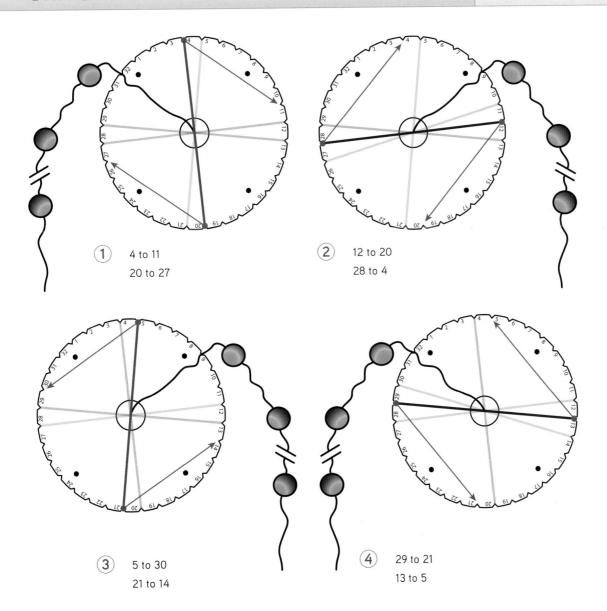

(1)   4 to 11

       20 to 27

(2)   12 to 20

       28 to 4

(3)   5 to 30

       21 to 14

(4)   29 to 21

       13 to 5

Braid around the rattail for approximately 4 inches, then start braiding around the first acrylic bead. When braiding around the beads, keep your interlacements loose (i.e., do not pull at all).

If you are having difficulty braiding around the acrylic beads, try one or both of these tricks:

(1) When you are ready to braid around a bead, add some weight to the completed braid. The weight will pull the braid down through the hole and stretch the interlacements, thus making room for the bead.

(2) Suspend the rattail with the beads high above the disk and make sure there is no slack (page 44). This should prevent the bead from sliding out of the braid as you work around it.

End caps attached to braid and closure (clasp).

Once you have braided around a bead, go back to braiding around the rattail for 1½ inches. Make sure you are now pulling tight around the rattail. Repeat to the end.

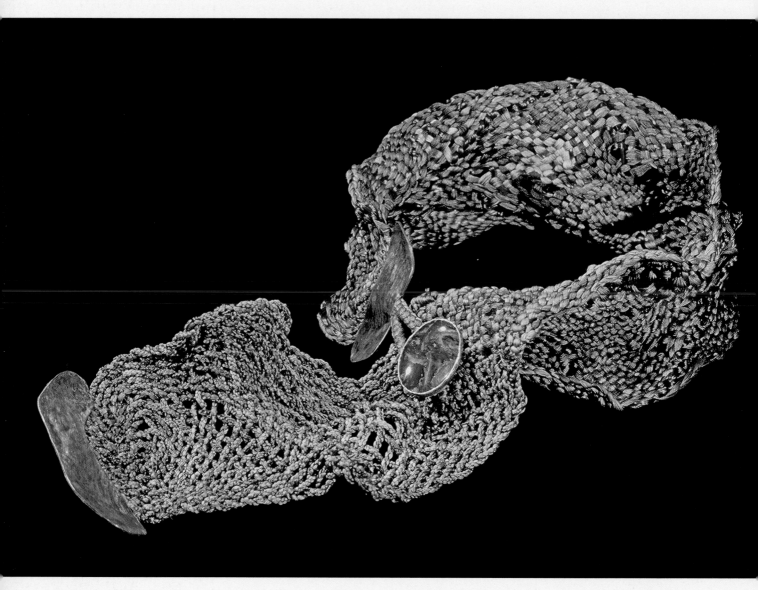

Neckpiece by Giovanna Imperia. This piece was braided with hand-dyed silk and copper wire and was executed on two stands: the Taka Dai and the Maru Dai. The focal point is a cabochon called moss agate. The silk was dyed to evoke the various shades and tones of moss.

WIRE + PLASTIC NECKLACE

For this project we will use the four-bundle structure called Maru Yatsu. While this is a very simple structure, consistent tension is extremely important in order to have even interlacements. This is particularly true of the braids made out of Jelly Yarn, which is slightly stretchy.

WHAT YOU'LL NEED

- 30-gauge (0.25 mm) coated copper wire:

    Amethyst: 1 bundle of 20 wires per slot x 4 slots x 32 inches (81 cm) per wire = 71 yards (65 m)

- Jelly Yarn:

    Ice, fine gauge: 1 yarn per slot x 4 slots x 38 inches (1 m) per yarn x 3 braids = 13 yards (12 m)

- Tools and supplies for measuring and setting up wire (page 21)

- Finishing tools and supplies for Finishing Technique #2 (page 47)

- 1 large (approximately 20 mm x 11 mm) oval end cap

- Toggle clasp of your choice

- 1 2½-inch (6.4 cm) length of Hill Tribes bent sterling silver tubing, 6mm (¼-inch) diameter

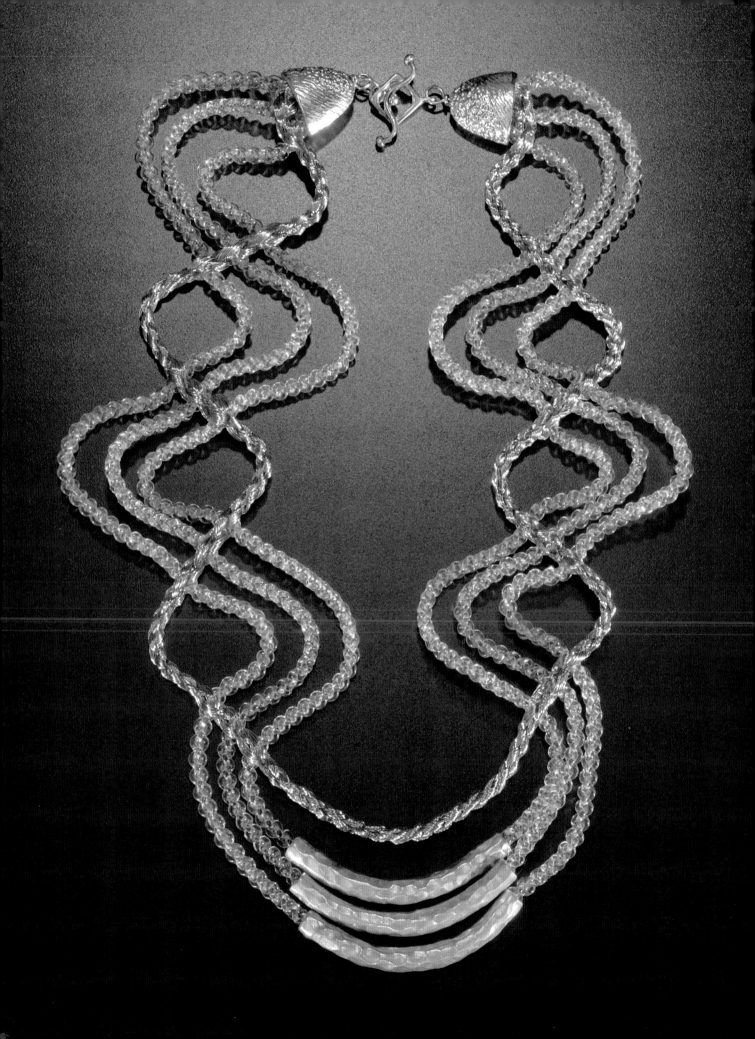

GETTING READY

There are two parts to this project: (1) You will make three separate braids with the Jelly Yarn, and then (2) you will incorporate these Jelly Yarn (plastic) braids into the wire braid. Once you complete the three plastic braids, measure the wire. Tie together the beginning of the wire to be braided with one end of the three plastic braids and then set up your disk as usual. It is important to rest the three plastic braids on the top of the disk (as shown), as you will need to move them in a specific order.

+ TIP

When braiding with plastic, make sure not to pull too tightly; plastic is stretchy, and pulling will deform the braid.

BRAIDING THE PLASTIC BRAIDS

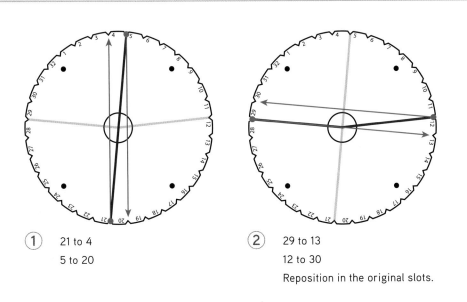

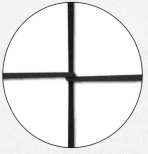

Point of braiding.

(1) 21 to 4
     5 to 20

(2) 29 to 13
     12 to 30
     Reposition in the original slots.

You should end up with three 29-inch-long braids. Slide each braid into the silver tubing and center the tube. Tie one end of the three braids with the wire with some yarn. This is a temporary tie to help you keep all the braids organized.

BRAIDING THE WIRE WITH THE PLASTIC BRAIDS

Place your three plastic braids (represented by the green lines labeled A, B, and C in the diagrams below) in the upper right section of your disk. Rest them on (do not place them into) slots 8–10. You will move them from the upper-right section (slots 8–10) to the lower-left section (slots 24–26) as you incorporate them into the wire braid structure. Be sure to read through all the written instructions that follow the diagrams before you begin braiding.

+ TIP

Once you start incorporating the plastic braids, remember to pull the wire consistently to ensure even interlacements

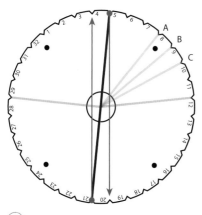

①   21 to 4
       5 to 20

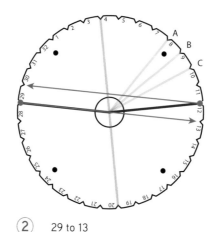

②   29 to 13
       12 to 30

Reposition in the original slots.

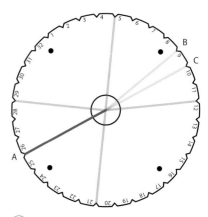

③   Move A from 8 to 26. Do Steps 1 and 2.

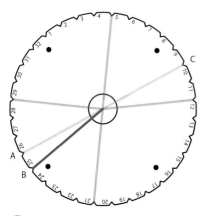

④   Move B from 9 to 25. Do Steps 1 and 2.

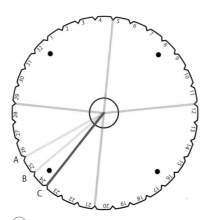

⑤   Move C from 10 to 24.

① Do Steps 1 and 2 a few times with the wire only. Do not move the plastic braids yet.

② Do Step 3, then Steps 1 and 2.

③ Do Step 4, then Steps 1 and 2.

④ Do Step 5.

⑤ Do Steps 1 and 2 seven times without moving the plastic braids.

⑥ You are now ready to move the plastic braids again. Follow this sequence:

     Move C from 24 to 10. Do Steps 1 and 2.

     Move B from 25 to 9. Do Steps 1 and 2

     Move A from 26 to 8

⑦ Do Steps 1 and 2 *seven times* without passing the plastic braids.

(8) Repeat text instructions 2–6 (above) *two times*, moving the plastic braids either to left or the right of the disk, according to the sequence above. You should have moved the plastic braids a total of *four times*. Now you have completed one side of the necklace.

(9) Do Steps 1 and 2 *sixteen times* without moving the plastic braids. This is the center of your necklace.

(10) You are now ready to start the other side of the necklace. Before you start moving the plastic braids, make sure that they are stacked one on top of the other and that the silver bent tubes are centered.

(11) Follow text instructions 2–6 (above) four times, moving the plastic braids either to the left or the right of the disk.

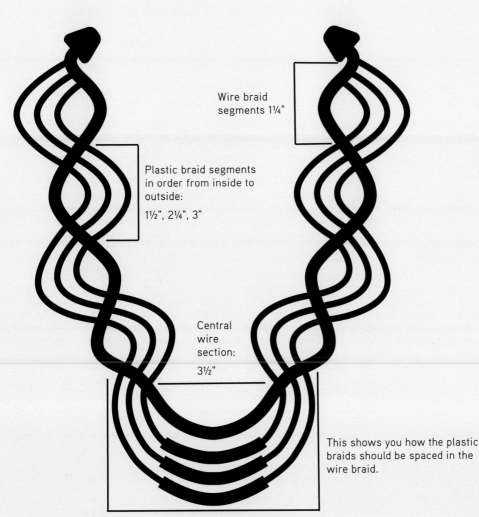

Wire braid segments 1¼"

Plastic braid segments in order from inside to outside:
1½", 2¼", 3"

Central wire section:
3½"

This shows you how the plastic braids should be spaced in the wire braid.

Central plastic braids sections in order from inside to outside:
4", 6", 7½"

FINISHING

You will use Finishing Technique #2 (page 47).

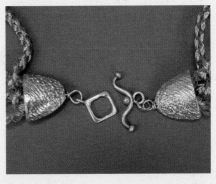

End caps attached to braid and closure (clasp).

Bracelet by Dominique Brochard.

PROJECTS on the
SQUARE PLATE

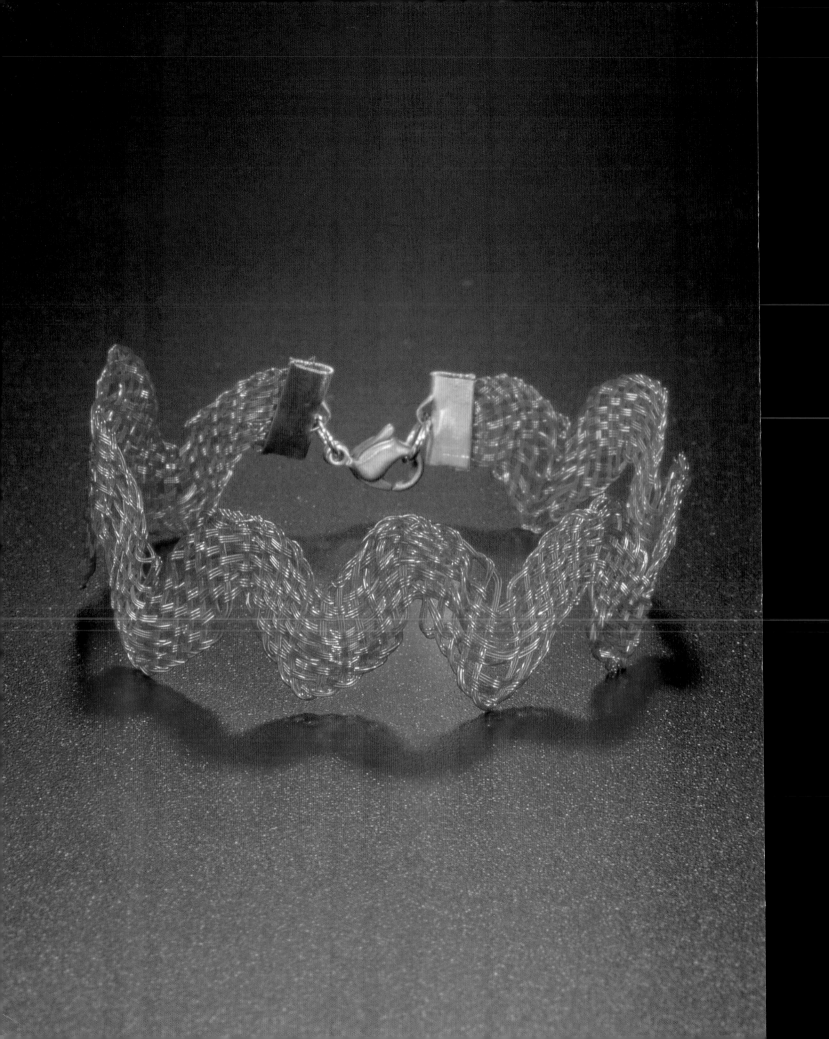

ZIGZAG BRACELET

The basic structure for the plate is a twelve-bundle Anda pattern. You create the zigzag effect by rotating the plate 180 degrees. See pages 36–38 for more details.

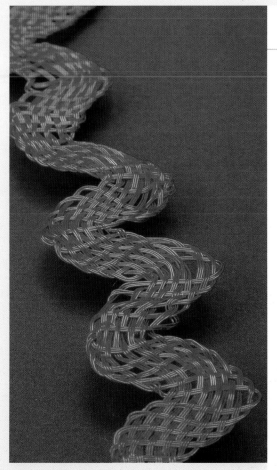

WHAT YOU'LL NEED

- 32-gauge (0.20 mm) coated copper wire:

  Tangerine: 1 bundle of 3 wires x 12 slots x 15 inches (37.5 cm) per wire = 37.5 yards (34 m)

- Tools and supplies for measuring and setting up wire (page 21)

- Finishing supplies for Finishing Technique #1 (page 46)

- 2 flat gold (color) end caps

- Gold (color) clasp

- Flat-nose pliers

+ **TIP**
To have a sharp edge when you rotate the plate, make sure you pull tight at Steps 4 and 11.

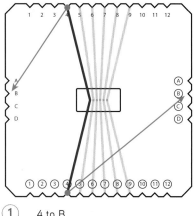

① 4 to B

④ to Ⓑ

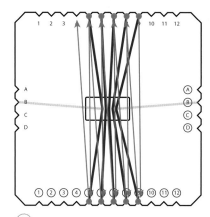

② Ⓢ to 4; 5 to ⑤

Ⓢ to 5; 6 to ⑥

Ⓢ to 6; 7 to ⑦

Ⓢ to 7; 8 to ⑧

Ⓢ to 8; 9 to ⑨

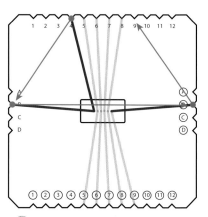

③ Ⓑ to 9

B to Ⓑ

4 to B

Repeat Steps 2 and 3 *four* times.

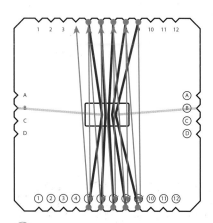

④ Ⓢ to 4; 5 to ⑤

Ⓢ to 5; 6 to ⑥

Ⓢ to 6; 7 to ⑦

Ⓢ to 7; 8 to ⑧

Ⓢ to 8; 9 to ⑨

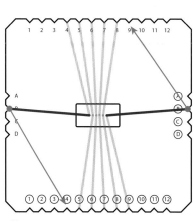

⑤ B to ④

Ⓑ to 9

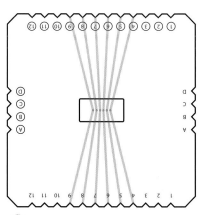

⑥ Rotate plate 180 degrees.

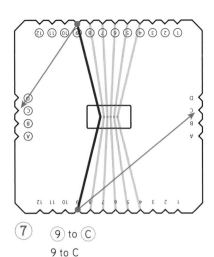

⑦ ⑨ to Ⓒ

9 to C

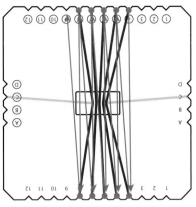

⑧ 8 to ⑨ ; ⑧ to 8
7 to ⑧ ; ⑦ to 7
6 to ⑦ ; ⑥ to 6
5 to ⑥ ; ⑤ to 5
4 to ⑤ ; ④ to 4

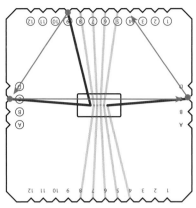

⑨ Ⓒ to ④
Ⓒ to C
⑨ to Ⓒ

Repeat Steps 8 and 9 *four*
times.

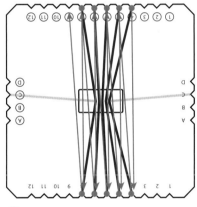

⑩ 8 to ⑨ ; ⑧ to 8
7 to ⑧ ; ⑦ to 7
6 to ⑦ ; ⑥ to 6
5 to ⑥ ; ⑤ to 5
4 to ⑤ ; ④ to 4

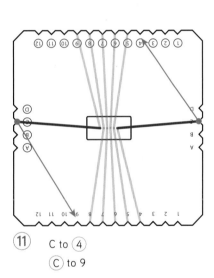

⑪ Ⓒ to ④
Ⓒ to 9

⑫ Rotate plate 180 degrees.
Go back to Step 1 and repeat
through Step 11.

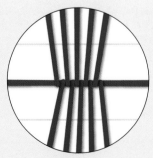

Point of braiding.

FINISHING

Once you have finished the braid, you can manipulate it to emphasize the zigzag effect. Use Finishing
Technique 2 (page 47). Use the flat-nose pliers to
tighten the end cap around the braid.

End caps attached to braid and closure (clasp).

RAFFIA + WIRE NECKLACE

This twenty-bundle flat braid is a variation of the Une braid (page 37). The interesting characteristic of this braid is that wire bundles are always kept in the center of the braid, where they form a ridge. The combination of the wire spine and the stiffer raffia makes it a shapeable necklace.

WHAT YOU'LL NEED

- Raffia:

    1 raffia thread per slot x 16 slots x 27 inches (68 cm) per thread = 12 yards (10.9 m)

- 30-gauge (0.25 mm) coated copper wire:

    Gold: 1 bundle of 4 wires per slot x 4 slots x 25 inches (63 cm) per wire = 11 yards (10 m)

- Tools and supplies for measuring and setting up wire (page 21)

- Finishing supplies for Finishing Technique #1 (page 46)

- 2 end caps with closure

- Masking tape

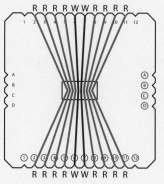

Color placement diagram.

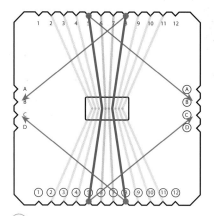

① 8 to B

5 to Ⓑ

⑧ to C

⑤ to Ⓒ

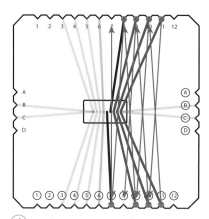

② Move 6 to 5; 7 to 8

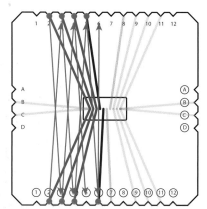

③ ⑥ to 6 and 5 to Ⓖ

④ to 5; 4 to ⑤

③ to 4; 3 to ④

② to 3; 2 to ③

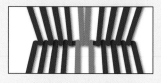

④ ⑦ to 7 and 8 to ⑦

⑨ to 8; 9 to ⑧

⑩ to 9; 10 to ⑨

⑪ to 10; 11 to ⑩

+ TIP

When you do Step 5, make sure you pull tight. You may find it easier to pull if you turn the plate 90 degrees.

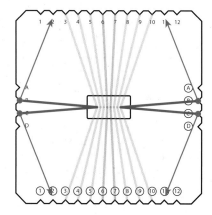

⑤ B to 2

C to ②

Ⓑ to 11

Ⓒ to ⑪

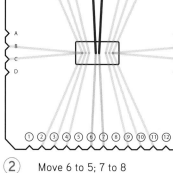

Point of braiding.

FINISHING

Because you are mixing fiber and wire, you will need to wrap the ends so that the fiber portion of the braid will not unravel. Take a small portion of masking tape and wrap it around the end of the braid. Trim the excess length. Use Finishing Technique #1 (page 46).

End caps attached to braid and closure (clasp).

Necklace by Anna Hurwitz in coated copper wire. It is interesting to see how Anna worked the two focal beads into the braid structure.

RUFFLED BRACELET

This project was done using the basic flat sixteen-bundle Anda braid (page 36). However, in this bracelet, half of the bundles consist of wire and the other half of thread. For every sequence of wire, you will do two in thread. This, combined with the fact that there is more thread than wire, will cause the braid to distort and ruffle.

WHAT YOU'LL NEED

- 30-gauge (0.25 mm) coated copper wire:

  Gold: 1 bundle of 3 wires per slot x 8 slots x 1 yard (90 cm) per wire = 24 yards (21.8 m)

- Thread (16/2 cotton, linen single, or size 10–12 crochet cotton):

  Black: 1 bundle of 6 threads per slot x 8 slots x 1½ yards (1.36 m) per thread = 72 yards (65.5 m)

- Tools and supplies for measuring and setting up wire and thread (page 21)

- Finishing tools and supplies for Finishing Technique #2 (page 47)

- 2 end caps

- Toggle clasp with closure

- Tapestry needle

GETTING STARTED

This braid has a lot of takeup, and the takeup is greater for the thread than the wire. Because the braid tends to twist and turn, you need to braid a longer braid to have enough ruffles in your bracelet. A number of variations are possible:

- You can increase the width of the braid by going from sixteen to twenty-four slots (still equally divided between wire and thread).

- You can emphasize the ruffles even more by doing three or four sequences just with thread before braiding the thread and wire together.

- You can reduce the number of wire bundles.

Point of braiding.

+ **TIP**

When you go back to Step 1, it is very important that you pull on the bundles in B and ⒝ very hard. The harder you pull, the more the braided fiber will curl.

BRAIDING THE BRACELET

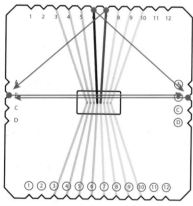

①   7 to B

     6 to ⒝

     Exchange B and ⒝

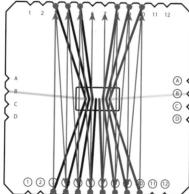

②   ⑥ to 6; 5 to ⑥

     ⑤ to 5; 4 to ⑤

     ⑤ to 4; 3 to ④

     ③ to 3

     ⑦ to 7; 8 to ⑦

     ⑧ to 8; 9 to ⑧

     ⑨ to 9; 10 to ⑨

     ⑩ to 10

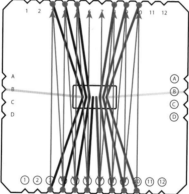

③   B to ③

     ⒝ to 10

     6 to B

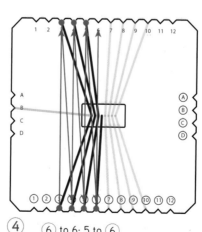

④   ⑥ to 6; 5 to ⑥

     ⑤ to 5; 4 to ⑤

     ⑤ to 4; 3 to ④

     ③ to 3

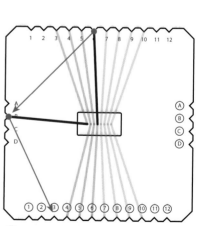

⑤   B to ③

     6 to B

     Repeat Steps 4 and then 5.
     Then go back to step 1.

FINISHING

Because you are mixing thread and wire, you will need to wrap the ends so that the thread does not unravel. Take a length of the same thread you used for braiding, fold it in half, and make a half hitch knot (page 43) around the braid. Wrap the excess thread around the braid. Insert the tails of the tie under the wrap with a tapestry needle. Use Finishing Technique #2 (page 47).

End caps attached to braid and closure (clasp).

Double layer Taka Dai braid by Giovanna Imperia. The top layer consists of just a few bundles of wire that form a leaf pattern of linked floats. Because the pattern is in the center of the braid, the flat structure was domed by hand in the center to highlight the design.

CHEVRON BRACELET + RING

This is a thick, flat twenty-four-bundle braid. The main challenge is the thickness of the wire. To have a closed structure, it is important to pull very tightly, particularly during the first move, where the central wire bundles are crossed and moved to the side slots. If not pulled tightly, there will be a small hole in the center. The stiffness of the wire may require you to slow down a bit to ensure consistent tension and even selvages (edges).

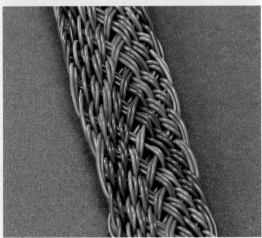

WHAT YOU'LL NEED

- 26-gauge (0.40 mm) coated copper wire:

  Lavender: 1 bundle of 2 wires per slot x 4 slots x 20 inches (25 cm) per wire = 4.4 yards (4 m)

  Turquoise: 1 bundle of 2 wires per slot x 4 slots x 20 inches (25 cm) per wire = 4.4 yards (4 m)

  Grape: 1 bundle of 2 wires per slot x 8 slots x 20 inches (25 cm) per wire = 8.8 yards (8 m)

  Powder blue: 1 bundle of 2 wires per slot x 8 slots x 20 inches (25 cm) per wire = 8.8 yards (8 m)

- Tools and supplies for measuring and setting up wire (page 21)

- Finishing tools and supplies for Finishing Techniques #1 (page 46)

- Finishing tools and supplies for Finishing Technique #4 (page 49)

- 1 ¼-inch (6.3 mm) length of sterling silver tubing, 8 mm (.31 inch) internal diameter

- 2 flat end caps with closure

125

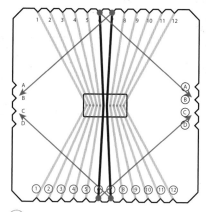

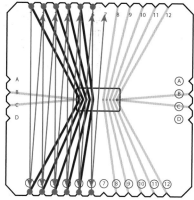

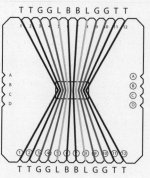

①
6 to Ⓑ
7 to B
⑥ to Ⓒ
⑦ to C

②
⑤ to 6; 5 to ⑥
④ to 5; 4 to ⑤
③ to 4; 3 to ④
② to 3; 2 to ③
① to 2; 1 to ②

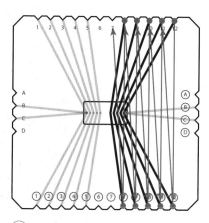

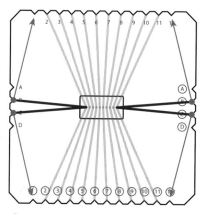

③
⑧ to 7; 8 to ⑦
⑨ to 8; 9 to ⑧
⑩ to 9; 10 to ⑨
⑪ to 10; 11 to ⑩
⑫ to 11; 12 to ⑪

④
C to ① ; B to 1
Ⓒ to ⑫ ; Ⓑ to 12

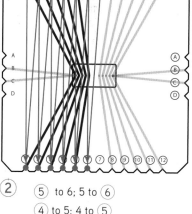

Color placement.

Point of braiding.

FINISHING

Tap the braid lightly with the mallet and wood block to get a smoother surface. Cut approximately 6½ inches (16 cm) for the bracelet and use the rest for the ring. Use Finishing Technique #2 (page 47) for the bracelet. Flatten a short section of the sterling silver tubing (approximately ¼ inch [10mm]) as in Finishing Technique #4 (page 49) and glue the ends inside the tubing.

End caps attached to braid and closure (clasp).   Flattened tube for ring.

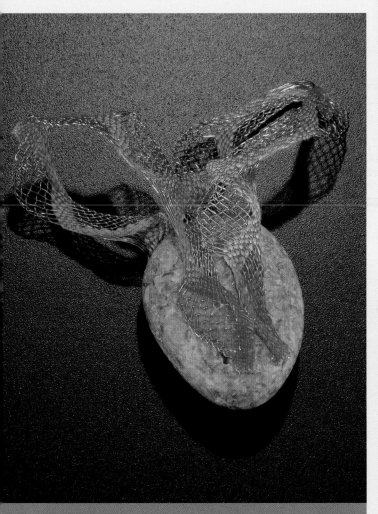

Pendant by Leigh Morris. It is interesting to note the different density of the fiber portion of the braid compared with the wire portion.

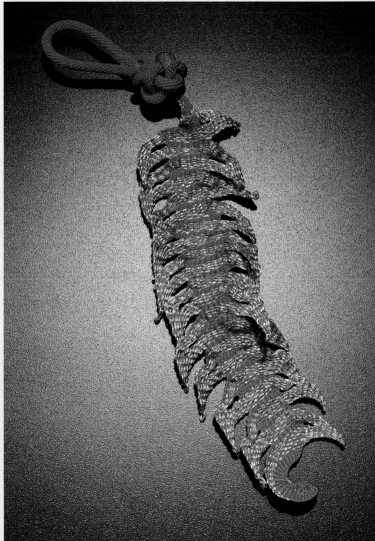

Bracelet by Dominique Brochard. In this zigzag braid, Dominique mixes threads and metallics. Note the loop closure, which is an extension of the rusty silk used in the main piece. Also note the Turk's Hat knot used as part of the closure.

SPIRAL BROOCH

This is another variation on the Anda braid (page 36), made with twelve bundles. To make the flat Anda spiral, we are borrowing the concept of short rows from knitting. Short rows allow you to make curves by partially braiding an existing row without changing the overall appearance of the braid. Once all the stitches are worked again, the braid will pull in and curve into a spiral.

WHAT YOU'LL NEED

- 30-gauge (0.25 mm) coated copper wire:

  Natural: 1 bundle of 5 wires per slot x 12 slots x 20 inches (50 cm) per wire = 33 yards (30 m)

- 16- or 18-gauge (1.3–1 mm) sterling silver or brass wire: 8-inch length

- Tools and supplies for measuring and setting up wire (page 21)

- Tools and supplies for Finishing Technique #2 (page 47)

- 2 gold end caps

- Ball-peen hammer

- Steel plate or small anvil

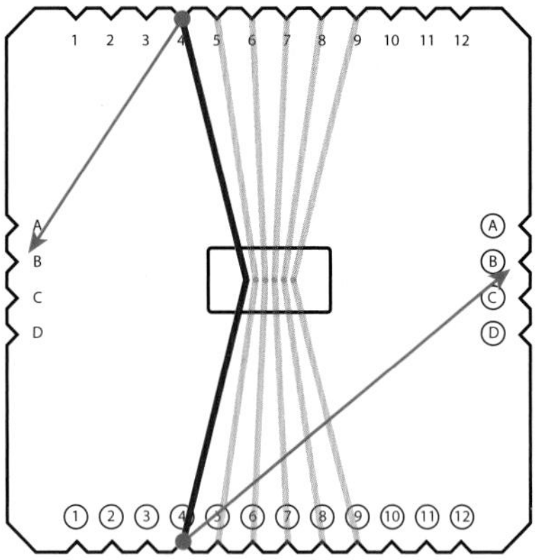

① 4 to B; ④ to Ⓑ

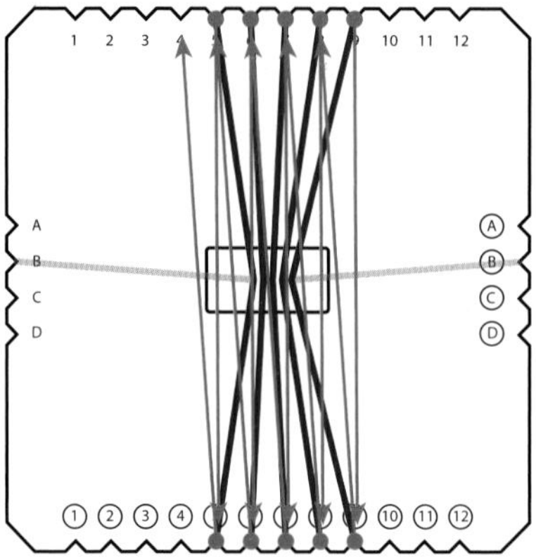

②
⑤ to 4; 5 to ⑤
⑥ to 5; 6 to ⑥
⑦ to 6; 7 to ⑦
⑧ to 7; 8 to ⑧
⑨ to 8; 9 to ⑨

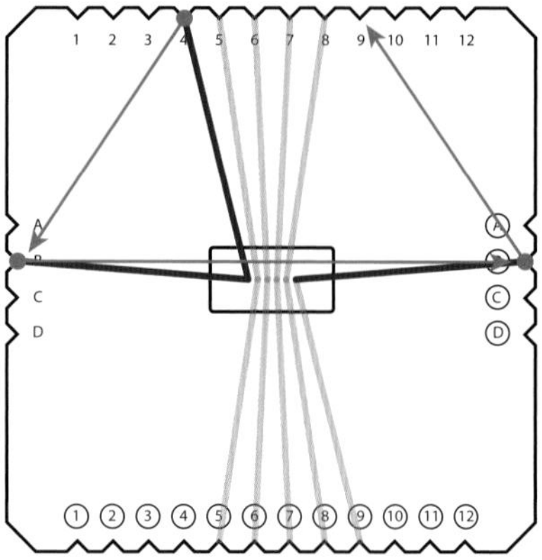

③
Ⓑ to 9; B to Ⓑ
4 to Ⓑ
Repeat Steps 2 and 3 *three* times.

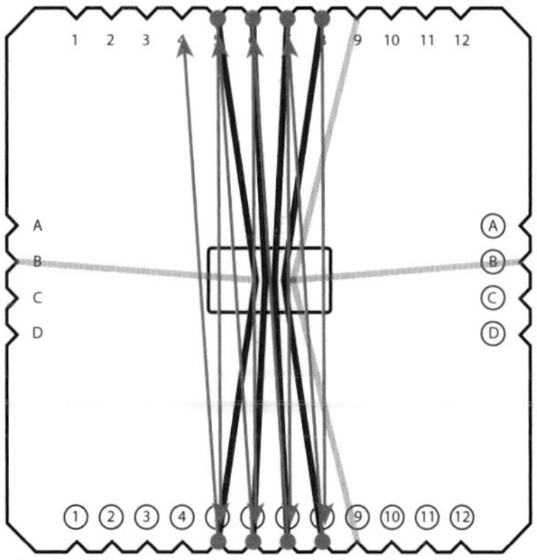

④
⑤ to 4; 5 to ⑤
⑥ to 5; 6 to ⑥
⑦ to 6; 7 to ⑦
⑧ to 7; 8 to ⑧

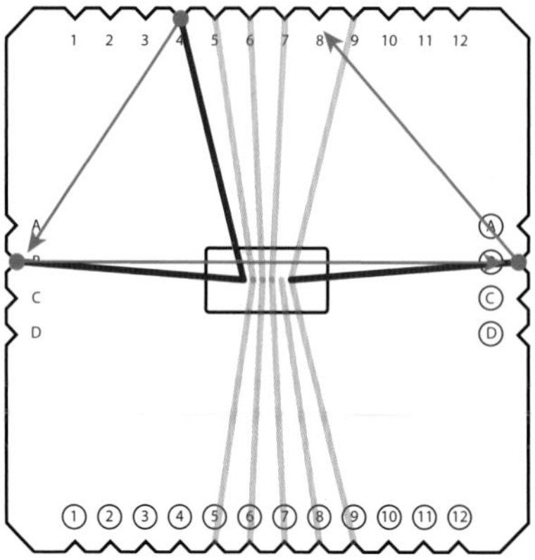

⑤
Ⓑ to 8; B to Ⓑ
4 to B

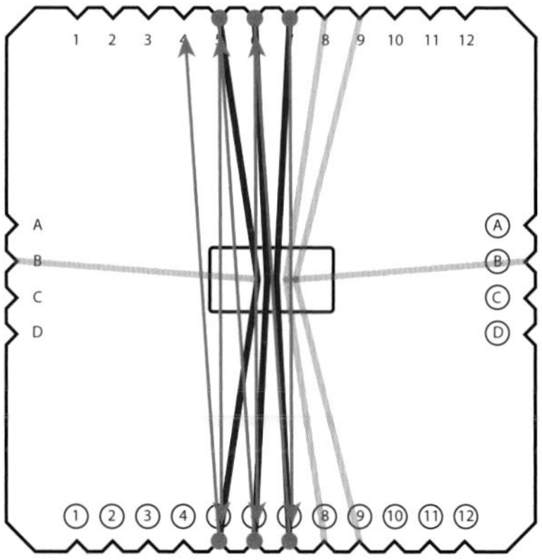

⑥
⑤ to 4; 5 to ⑤
⑥ to 5; 6 to ⑥
⑦ to 6; 7 to ⑦

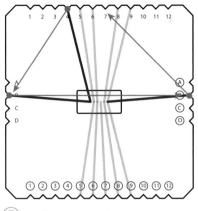

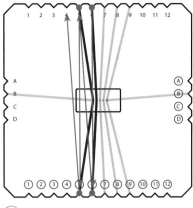

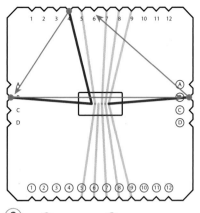

⑦ Ⓑ to 7; B to Ⓑ
4 to B

⑧ ⑤ to 4; 5 to ⑤
⑥ to 5; 6 to ⑥

⑨ Ⓑ to 6; B to Ⓑ
4 to Ⓑ

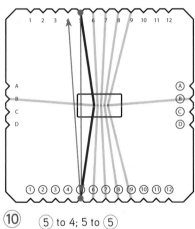

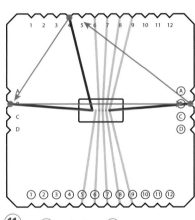

⑩ ⑤ to 4; 5 to ⑤

⑪ Ⓑ to 5; B to Ⓑ
4 to B

Steps 2 and 3 alone create a straight Anda braid. Repeat Steps 2 and 3 for about 1 inch. This will give you a good length of straight braid that will be inserted in the end caps. Then start the spiral (Steps 3–11). Repeat Steps 2–11 until you have 3–4 inches of wire left.

With the remaining wire, repeat Steps 2 and 3 until you have about 1 inch of straight braid. It will take a few rounds before the braid will start visibly spiraling.

SHORT ROWS

In Step 2 you are exchanging all the wires in N and S. In Step 4 you are exchanging one less, in Step 7 two less, and so on. These are short rows. It will take a few rounds before the braid visibly spirals.

FINISHING

Finish the braid using Finishing Technique #2 (page 47), but here you will only need the end caps, not the clasps. Once you have finished the braid, manipulate it to emphasize the spiraling effect.

+ **TIP**

When you are doing short rows, some threads remain stationary longer than others. To have a good spiral, it is very important that, after completing Step 11 and then Step 2, you pull your wires very tight. The tighter you pull, the more the braid will spiral.

Completed short-row sequence. The wires get longer as you go from the left to the right of the plate, because you stopped exchanging wires from the right.

ADDING THE STERLING SILVER OR BRASS WIRE CLASP

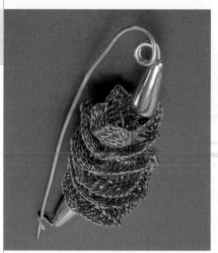

Closed clasp and double loop (at top of brooch).

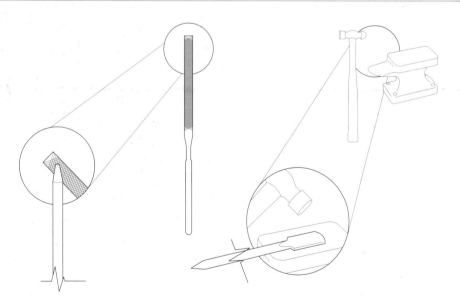

① Using the mill file, file one end of the sterling silver or brass wire to a point. *Do not bend the wire yet!*

② Lay the wire on the steel plate or small anvil and, with the ball-peen hammer, flatten about ½ inch of the opposite (not filed) end. Be careful not to make it too thin. If needed, use your file to round the edges.

③ Take the braid and gently slide the pointed end of the wire through the end cap, through the entire length of the braid, until it comes out through the end cap at the other end of the braid.

④ Use your round-nose pliers to make a bend in the flattened wire at one end of the braid and chain-nose pliers to make a square bend in the wire at the opposite end. Set the finished brooch aside for 24 hours to allow the glue to be fully cured.

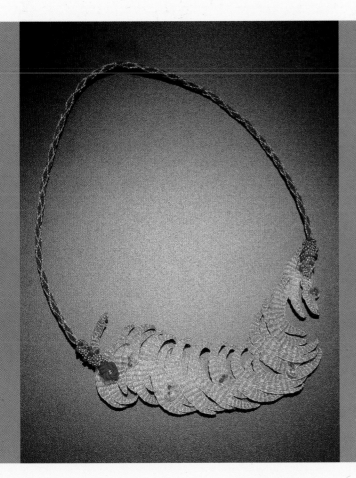

Necklace by Dominique Brochard. The neckpiece is coated copper wire and fiber braided on the disk. The centerpiece is metallic braided on the square plate.

SQUARE BROOCH

As with the Spiral Brooch, this braid also uses the concept of short rows (page 132), but this brooch uses sixteen bundles (not twelve). Another difference is that the short rows here are worked slightly differently, resulting in sharper corners. If the same sequence is repeated over and over (four to five times), the braid will form a square spiral (or a spiral with corners). But if, as in this project, the plate is turned 180 degrees, the direction of the spiral will turn, resulting in a more organic, less geometric form.

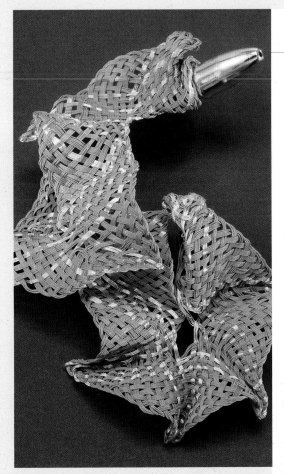

WHAT YOU'LL NEED

- 32-gauge (0.02 mm) coated copper wire:

  Non-tarnish silver: 1 bundle of 5 wires per slot x 4 slots x 25 inches (63 cm) per wire = 14 yards (12.6 m)

  Gray: 1 bundle of 5 wires per slot x 12 slots x 25 inches (63 cm) per wire = 41.6 yards (37.9 m)

- 18-gauge sterling silver or steel wire: approximately 7 inches (17.5 cm)

- Tools and supplies for measuring and setting up wire (page 21)

- Finishing tools and supplies for Finishing Technique #3 (page 48)

- 2 silver or silver-plated end caps

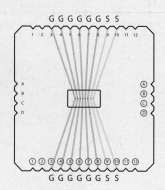

G G G G G G S S

Color placement.

Note: Colors will change positions as you repeat Steps 1–30. Therefore, the diagrams used in the directions section have been kept as a single color to reduce confusion.

G G G G G G S S

+ TIPS

Be sure to read through all the instructions before you start braiding.

For details on short rows, see the Spiral Brooch project on page 129.

BRAIDING THE BROOCH

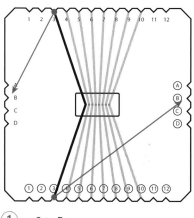

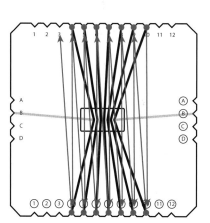

① 3 to B
③ to Ⓑ

② ④ to 3; 4 to ④
⑤ to 4; 5 to ⑤
⑥ to 5; 6 to ⑥
⑦ to 6; 7 to ⑦
⑧ to 7; 8 to ⑧
⑨ to 8; 9 to ⑨
⑩ to 9; 10 to ⑩

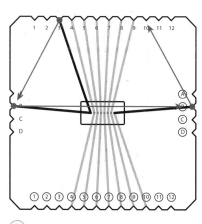

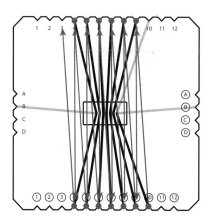

③ Ⓑ to 10
B to Ⓑ
3 to B

④ ④ to 3; 4 to ④
⑤ to 4; 5 to ⑤
⑥ to 5; 6 to ⑥
⑦ to 6; 7 to ⑦
⑧ to 7; 8 to ⑧
⑨ to 8; 9 to ⑨
⑩ to 9

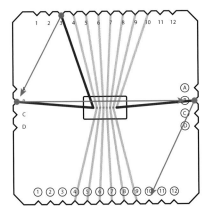

(5)   (B) to (10)
B to (B)
3 to B

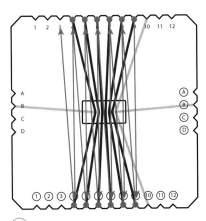

(6)   (4) to 3; 4 to (4)
(5) to 4; 5 to (5)
(6) to 5; 6 to (6)
(7) to 6; 7 to (7)
(8) to 7; 8 to (8)
(9) to 8; 9 to (9)

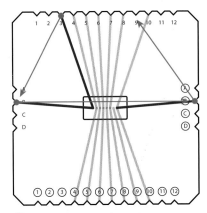

(7)   (B) to 9
B to (B)
3 to B

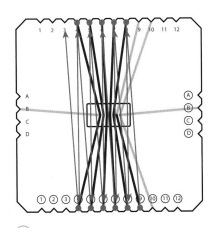

(8)   (4) to 3; 4 to (4)
(5) to 4; 5 to (5)
(6) to 5; 6 to (6)
(7) to 6; 7 to (7)
(8) to 7; 8 to (8)
(9) to 8

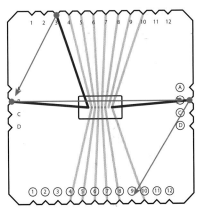

(9)   (B) to 9
B to (B)
3 to B

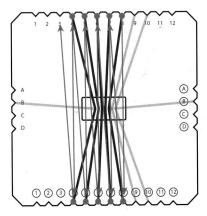

(10)   (4) to 3; 4 to (4)
(5) to 4; 5 to (5)
(6) to 5; 6 to (6)
(7) to 6; 7 to (7)
(8) to 7; 8 to (8)

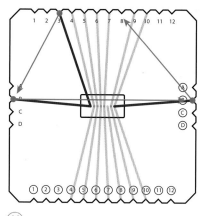

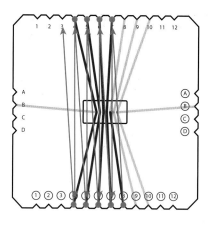

12
④ to 3; 4 to ④
⑤ to 4; 5 to ⑤
⑥ to 5; 6 to ⑥
⑦ to 6; 7 to ⑦
⑧ to 7

11
Ⓑ to 8
B to Ⓑ
3 to B

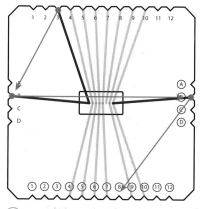

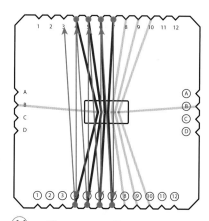

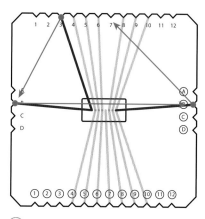

13
Ⓑ to ⑧
B to Ⓑ
3 to B

14
④ to 3; 4 to ④
⑤ to 4; 5 to ⑤
⑥ to 5; 6 to ⑥
⑦ to 6; 7 to ⑦

15
Ⓑ to 7
B to Ⓑ
3 to B

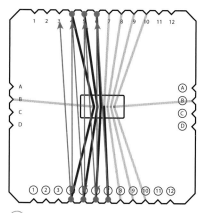

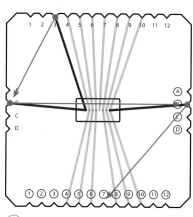

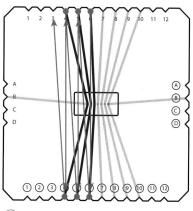

16
④ to 3; 4 to ④
⑤ to 4; 5 to ⑤
⑥ to 5; 6 to ⑥
⑦ to 6

17
B to ⑦
B to Ⓑ
3 to B

18
④ to 3; 4 to ④
⑤ to 4; 5 to ⑤
⑥ to 5; 6 to ⑥

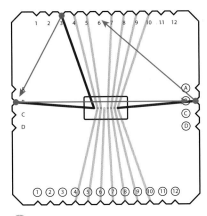

19 (B) to 6
B to (B)
3 to B

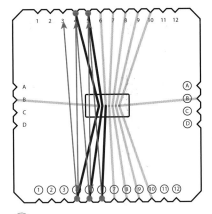

20 (4) to 3; 4 to (4)
(5) to 4; 5 to (5)
(6) to 5

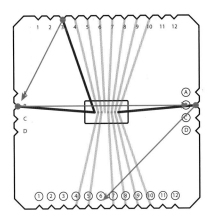

21 B to (6)
B to (B)
3 to B

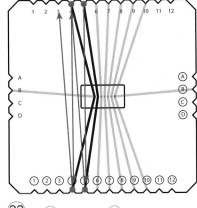

22 (4) to 3; 4 to (4)
(5) to 4; 5 to (5)

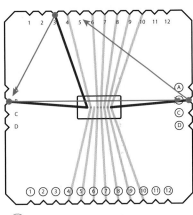

23 (B) to 5
B to (B)
3 to B

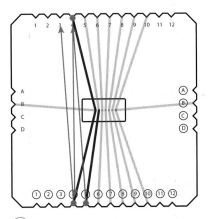

24 (4) to 3; 4 to (4)
(5) to 4

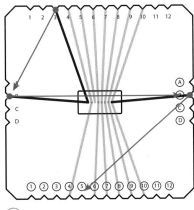

25 (B) to 5
B to (B)
3 to B

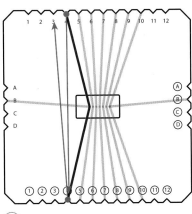

26 (4) to 3; 4 to (4)

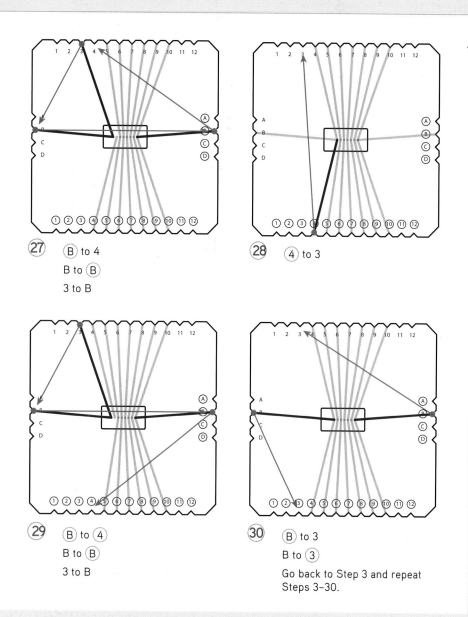

(27) (B) to 4
B to (B)
3 to B

(28) (4) to 3

(29) (B) to (4)
B to (B)
3 to B

(30) (B) to 3
B to (3)
Go back to Step 3 and repeat
Steps 3–30.

TIP

When you are going back to Step 1, make sure you are pulling tight on all the wires so that there are no gaps.

If you keep repeating Steps 1–30, you will have a square spiral. However, it is possible to change the direction in which the spiral turns by rotating the plate 180 degrees, similar to what you would do for a zigzag braid (pages 114–115).

As you can see from the photo above, I changed direction of the spiral for this brooch. I first braided Steps 1–30 *five times* with the plate in the correct orientation (the circled numbers in the S position). I then turned the plate 180 degrees so the circled numbers were in the N position. I then braided Steps 1–30 *five times* again.

You may find this a bit challenging, but the key is to pay attention to the moves rather than the numbers. As you go through Steps 1–30, you'll notice that you stop exchanging the N and S wires from the right side of the plate in this order: 10, (10), 9, (9), 8, (8), 7, (7), etc. When you turn the plate 180 degrees, the lower numbers will be on your right side (1, 2, 3, 4, etc.). Therefore, you will stop exchanging between N and S slots in this order: (3), 3, (4), 4, (5), 5, (6), 6, etc.

FINISHING

Shape the braid until you find a form you like by compressing and twisting the spiraling sections. Use Finishing Technique #2 to place the end caps. Once the glue is set, bend the ends of the braid so that the end caps face each other.

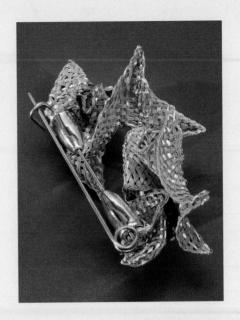

ADDING THE STERLING SILVER WIRE PINBACK

(1) With mill file, file one end of the 18-gauge silver wire to a point; bend wire in half with chain-nose pliers. With the round-nose pliers, make a loop. Now the two halves of the wire are in a straight line.

(2) With the round-nose pliers, make another loop. Now the two halves of the wire are parallel. Gently insert the half of the wire with the dull point through the end caps now.

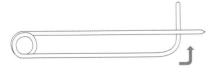

(3) With the chain-nose pliers make a 90-degree bend in the wire that you just inserted through the end caps, approximately ½ inch from the end.

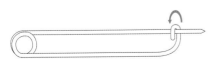

(4) With the flat-nose pliers fold the bent end over the wire with the sharp point.

RESOURCES

C-LON
www.caravanbeads.com

www.agrainofsand.com

Local bead store

COLOR PIGMENTS AND FINISHING SPRAY
Local art supply store

Local craft store

END CAPS
www.riogrande.com

www.metalliferous.com

www.philipjmertens.com (Hill Tribes silver)

www.ornabead.com

Local bead shops

EPOXY RESIN
Local hardware store (Devcon 2-ton clear)

www.sherrihaab-shop.com (Ice resin)

EZ BOBS
www.braidershand.com

www.giovannaimperiadesigns.com

www.ebay.com

FELT BALLS
www.ornamentea.com

www.giovannaimperiadesigns.com

FINISHING TOOLS
www.riogrande.com

www.metalliferous.com

www.ottofrei.com

www.micromark.com

Local jewelry supply store

FISHING WEIGHTS
Any outdoor sport/fishing goods store

HAMANAKA BRAND DISKS AND SQUARE PLATES
www.braidershand.com

www.giovannaimperiadesigns.com

www.ebay.com

JELLY YARN®
www.jellyyarn.com

www.giovannaimperiadesigns.com

KUMIHIMO BOOKS
www.braidershand.com

www.unicornbooks.com

www.careycompany.com

www.giovannaimperiadesigns.com

KUMIHIMO STANDS
www.braidershand.com

www.careycompany.com

www.kumiday.co.uk

www.shirleyberlin.com

www.majacraft.co.nz

PRECUT COPPER STRIPS
www.metalliferous.com

SEED BEADS
www.caravanbeads.com

www.firemountaingems.com

www.ornabead.com

www.genbead.com

Local bead shops

SILVER TUBING, SILVER WIRE
www.riogrande.com

www.metalliferous.com

www.ottofrei.com

TAPESTRY NEEDLES, SCISSORS
Local fabric or craft store

VINTAGE ACRYLIC BEADS
www.ornabead.com

www.vintagebeadsandmore.com

www.agrainofsand.com

www.ebay.com

WIRE
www.beadalon.com
(worldwide web and retail presence)

www.wire.co.uk

www.riogrande.com

www.metalliferous.com

www.giovannaimperiadesigns.com

FURTHER READING

MARU DAI
Berlin, Shirley and Goodwin, Carol: *Sixty Sensational Samples – a Kumihimo Collection*. Self-published, USA 2004

Carey, Jacqui: *Beads and Braids*. Carey Company, UK 1999

Carey, Jacqui: *Creative Kumihimo*. Carey Company, UK 1994

Domyo School: *Kumihimo Manual*. Domyo, Japan 1976

Kakimoto, Kumiko: *Dream Braiding*. Self-published, Japan 1995

Martin, Catherine: *Kumihimo—Japanese Silk Braiding Techniques*. Lark Books, USA 1986

Morris, Leigh: *A Chameleon Braid*. Self-published, New Zealand 2005

Nakayama, Aya: *Kumihimo Jewelry*. Bijutsu Shuppan-Sha, Japan 1979

Owen, Rodrick: *250 Braids*. Interweave Press, USA 1995

Sakai Aiko and Tada, Makiko: *Kumihimo—the Essence of Japanese Braiding*. Vogue, Japan 1985

Tada, Makiko: *Comprehensive Treatise of Braids. Vol. 1: Maru Dai Braids*. Texte, Japan 1996

DISK AND SQUARE PLATE
Tada, Makiko: *Comprehensive Treatise of Braids. Vol.6: Round Disk and Square Plate Braids*. Texte, Japan 2007

LOOP MANIPULATION BRAIDING
Kinoshita, Masako: *Kute-Uchi Basic Techniques*. Self-published, Japan 2000

HISTORY AND THE JAPANESE AESTHETICS

Carey, Jacqui: *Braids and Beyond.* Carey Company, 2003

Carey, Jacqui: *Samurai Undressed.* Carey Company, 1995

Koren, Leonard: *Wabi-Sabi for Artists, Designers, Poets and Philosophers.* Stone Bridge Press, 1994

Sahashi, Kei: *Exquisite—the World of Japanese Kumihimo Braiding.* Kodansha International, Japan 1988

Shima, Yukiko: *A Step Into Kimono and Kumihimo.* International College of California, USA 1979

Speiser, Noemi: *The Manual of Braiding.* Speiser, Switzerland, 1983

Yamoka, Issei: *Kumihimo in Shosoin.* Heibunsha, Japan 1973

Yanagi, Soetsu: *The Unknown Craftsman—a Japanese Insight into Beauty.* Kodansha International, Japan 1972

WORKING WITH WIRE AND FINISHING TECHNIQUES

Fisch, Arline: *Textile Techniques in Metal.* Lark Books, USA 1996

Hettemansperger, Mary: *Wrap, Stitch, Fold and Rivet.* Lark Books, USA 2005

WIRE CONVERSION CHART

U.S. Gauge	American Wire Gauge (AWG) / Brown & Sharpe *Inches*	American Wire Gauge (AWG) *Metric*	Imperial Standard Wire Gauge (SWG) *Inches*	Imperial Standard Wire Gauge (SWG) *Metric*
18	0.0403	1.1024	0.048	1.219
20	0.032	0.8128	0.036	0.914
22	0.0253	0.6425	0.028	0.711
24	0.0201	0.5106	0.022	0.558
26	0.0159	0.4038	0.018	0.457
28	0.0126	0.32	0.0148	0.375
30	0.01	0.254	0.0124	0.314
32	0.008	0.2032	0.0108	0.274
34	0.0063	0.1601	0.0092	0.233
36	0.005	0.127	0.0076	0.193
38	0.004	0.1016	0.006	0.152
40	0.0031	0.0787	0.0048	0.121
42	0.0025	0.0635	0.004	0.101
44	0.002	0.0508	0.0032	0.081
46	0.0016	0.0406	0.0024	0.06

This chart compares the gauge normally used in the United States (AWG) with other standard measurements. In the UK, gauges are also used, but British gauge numbers (SWG) are slightly different than American gauges—that is, gauge 30 in the United States is actually finer than gauge 30 in the UK. Please refer to the metric or inch measurement to ensure that you are getting the correct size wire.